DYING
for a
DRINK

AMELIA BAKER

authorHOUSE®

AuthorHouse™ UK
1663 Liberty Drive
Bloomington, IN 47403 USA
www.authorhouse.co.uk
Phone: 0800.197.4150

*Scriptures taken from the Holy Bible, New International Version®, NIV®. Copyright ©
1973, 1978, 1984, 2011 by Biblica, Inc.™ Used by permission of Zondervan. All rights
reserved worldwide. www.zondervan.com The "NIV" and "New International Version" are
trademarks registered in the United States Patent and Trademark Office by Biblica, Inc.™*

Published by AuthorHouse 06/12/2018

ISBN: 978-1-5462-9378-1 (sc)
ISBN: 978-1-5462-9379-8 (hc)
ISBN: 978-1-5462-9377-4 (e)

Print information available on the last page.

This book is printed on acid-free paper.

CONTENTS

ACKNOWLEDGEMENTS

I would like to thank my two amazing kids, their dad, my family, and my wonderful friends, especially my three best ones. These people have loved, supported, and encouraged me through indescribably bad times.

To my dad, for never giving up on me, for encouraging
me, and loving me unconditionally.

INTRODUCTION

I don't believe I woke up one day when I was a little girl and thought, *When I grow up, I'd love to be a chronic alcoholic, cause chaos and devastation, and hurt all my loved ones, drive while drunk, be hospitalised several times as a result of alcohol misuse, and nearly die from either blackout falls or attempted suicide.* Here I am, fifty-two years old. I've been married twice, am single, and have two beautiful kids—a son, twenty-three, and a daughter, twenty. What used to be a loving and supportive family has been ripped apart through the consequences of my drinking.

I thought long and hard about writing *Dying for a Drink.* It's the truth, the whole truth, and nothing but the truth. I needed to seriously reduce 'waffle'. By that I mean, long descriptive stories describing amazing, fun times with family and friends and many other people who have been a part of my life. While I'm so grateful for these times and memories, I aim to expose addiction for what it really is and the 'insanity' that prevails— the definition of insanity being 'repeating the same thing and expecting a different outcome'. Different outcomes, yes, in my case, escalating to deadly heights and causing unimaginable fear and hurt to my loved ones.

Subsequently, the initial word count has been almost halved. This process proved difficult, as there was so much I wanted to say, a lot of which included apologies/explanations following every shocking event. By the end of my drinking, these events were so frequent that I decided that keeping them 'factual' would lead to any easier read and prevent distraction from the main aim.

The pain and shame of reliving the 'horrors' and the hurt I've caused loved has led me to stop writing for days on end in order to protect my recovery and sanity.

You shall hear me describe, in detail, my time in rehab in the UK, to 'set the scene', as it were. I've chosen not to talk in detail about the abundance of emotions I experienced. They swung radically on a daily basis, and I learnt they needed to be felt at a level I'd never experienced. I would like to apologise in advance if my use of humour proves offensive or appears to minimise the seriousness of this deadly disease. That is not my intention. I do, however, believe laughter is a wonderful God-given gift, and it's been a blessing during unimaginable dark times.

I've questioned myself time and time again if writing this was good idea. Did I really want my loved ones, especially my kids, to be exposed to the awful truths of my addiction? They've already suffered enough. My 'perfectionism' has been a big barrier. I don't consider myself an intellectual, and often I worried that my style of writing, which is basic and rather scrambled due to being back in early recovery again, could lead to it being heavily criticised. I've told myself 'so be it', as the only reason I'm writing this is in the hope it will help other alcoholics and drug addicts to identify and realise there is *hope*, no matter how horrendous your story is.

I suffer from a chronic, progressive, incurable, and often-fatal disease, which is centred in my mind. Personally, I find reading 'real stories' far more helpful than any textbook or self-help book. I do read five 'daily readings' books, all related to addiction and faith. It's a great way to start my day. I also hope *Dying for a Drink* will help anyone addicted to other things—gambling, sex, food, the Internet, shopping, love or relationships. I could go on, as there are many addictions.

By the grace of God, I haven't had a gambling problem. Actually, as I say that, I realise it's untrue. I've gambled with my life more times than I can count. I liken it to Russian roulette. I never knew if this would be the time I'd die or kill myself while drinking. I think that qualifies me as an extreme gambler! Please, as they say in AA (Alcoholics Anonymous), look out for the similarities, not the differences, in my story. You may well think as you read this, *What a privileged life she's had.* Yes, my life was financially privileged when my first husband worked his way up the corporate ladder. But as my Mum said, 'Money doesn't make you happy. It just makes a bad situation easier.' And though this is true, at the end of my drinking, I ended up barely existing—without self-worth, hating myself, and crippled with fear. I wanted to die and was unable to imagine life without alcohol or drugs.

Yes, drugs and alcohol took my pain away temporarily, but the day always came when I had to face the reality and consequences of my incredibly destructive thinking and behaviour. The pain got worse, and the only solution I could come up with was to 'medicate' my feelings away. This, in my case, happened over and over again. Maybe I'm a slow learner. I was desperate not to be an alcoholic, defiant in the extreme, and in total denial for many years.

I drank socially for many years. They were fun and happy times. No two stories are the same. Multiple stories can be very similar, but we addicts are 'unique' human beings, just like non-addicted people are unique. The only difference is, I believe, we are 'hard-wired' differently, which is why our family and friends often struggle with the idea that we are not bad people trying to be good. We are sick people trying to get well.

Often, the damage we have caused ourselves and our loved ones is so huge that reconciliation may never happen. The fortunate ones manage to get and remain clean and sober. Life starts to improve, and gradually over time, relationships heal, and trust is restored. The World Health Organisation acknowledges addiction as a mental illness, so we aren't imagining it! If we were suffering from another illness or disease, we would receive love, care, compassion, and support.

There is still a stigma attached to addiction. When I first heard it described as a disease, I thought it was a 'cop-out'; I was just a terrible person. My first AA sponsor broke it down into two words—*dis* and *ease*, a feeling of being uneasy. That made sense, but for me it didn't 'cut it'. I was way past feeling uneasy. I loathed myself and what I'd done, and the emotional pain was excruciating.

I'm going to be totally upfront about my faith now, but I urge you, if you have no faith or you have endured bad experiences relating to any types of church, do not slam the book shut and toss it in the bin. As a family, we attended the local Anglican church every Sunday morning, trying to look like 'the perfect middle-class family'. At eighteen I went to London to train as a nurse. Any faith I may have had vanished. I saw suffering and death and knew in my heart that there couldn't possibly be a God.

I became a Christian years later, when my son was about fourteen months old. He had been incredibly sick as a baby and needed radical surgery to save his kidneys. I wasn't sure who or what God was. It didn't matter. All I know is that I witnessed a miracle with our very sick child. He was three days post-op and had IVs, a supra-pubic catheter, and was being fed through a nasogastric tube. He was experiencing bladder cramps, which the nurse told me were 'like labour pains'. I am sure that any mum reading this can imagine my desperation as I watched him writhe around the cot. The painkillers weren't touching the pain. I was still breastfeeding him, more for comfort than anything else, as I had virtually no milk coming in. I felt alone and angry this was happening, and I barely slept or ate. One particularly bad night, he was crying so loudly that I cried out (not literally) to a God I didn't understand. *If you are real*, do *something*. Our son stopped crying, lay still, and looked totally peaceful. I looked on in amazement and had an overwhelming feeling that he was being cradled by Jesus. He recovered well, and we took him home a few days later.

Again *please* don't shut the book thinking I'm some Bible-thumping lunatic who prays in a 'holier than thou' voice. I've witnessed this many times and wondered why people do it. When I pray, I use the same voice I would use with a friend. It's just different—content. I feel safe, protected, and loved unconditionally. And I understand that God's desire for me is to become the best version of myself by surrendering to his will. My faith has been strong, weak, and non-existent at times since that day. Where I fall on that scale is directly linked to my state of mind and the amount I've drunk. When I refer to God, please, in your mind, think of your own higher power. If you don't have one yet, then may I suggest what I've heard suggested in AA—borrow someone else's. Just being in a meeting means you are not alone. You are surrounded by like-minded people, and many people make AA or other twelve-step programmes their higher power. The beauty of nature, the wonder of the universe, and other such things are also used successfully by many recovering addicts.

Everything I am writing comes from my heart; from living in chronic addiction; and from mixing with other addicts, therapists, and staff members in the rehabilitation centres I was in and through AA and other outside help. I would like to stress how essential the belief in a higher power is in order to get and remain clean and sober. One thing I know for certain is it can't be you or me.

When I first went to AA, a woman shared her story; it was heartbreaking, and I was shocked. I chatted with her after the meeting. I was still in denial, thinking I could stop if I really wanted to. What she said has stuck in my mind ever since, and I would like to share it, as it may help anyone who is in the place I was in all those years ago. She said, 'Don't let my story become yours.' Her words were short and a bit confusing at the time, as I knew I'd never end up like that. But guess what? Most of her story ended up being mine. I have loved my kids with all my heart and soul since the moment I held them in my arms for the first time, and will do so until the day I die. Alcohol hardened my heart. It was my *god* and became the only thing I cared about. Even my intense love for my kids could not keep me sober or prevent me from relapsing many times. That, to me, demonstrates the incredible power of addiction.

I would like to add that nothing written in this book is intended to blame or shame any of my loved ones. I've already done that in the extreme. My addiction led me to isolate, lie, and run on resentments and vengeful thoughts. As my disease progressed, the most destructive thing I did was to manipulate loved ones and situations, and I always needed to be *right*. Everyone has limits, and these relationships are 'fragile' at best because of me. I can only hope and pray, in time, healing will occur and trust will be restored.

I have learnt many things. One of the biggest revelations was that drink and drugs aren't the problem. The problem is *me*—the way I think, feel, and behave. I used to feel confused when I heard people share in AA that it was the first drink that did the damage. How ridiculous. I loved the first drink and believed it was the second or third bottle that caused the problems. In my final years of drinking, if I had one drink, I couldn't stop unless hospitalised or friends prompted me into rehab. My addiction hasn't killed me—*yet*. I know without any doubt that, if I choose to pick up a drink again, it won't be long before I'm dead. We all have choices. I choose *life*, and I hope and pray you will too after reading *Dying for a Drink*.

CHAPTER 1

MY LIFE BEFORE I CROSSED THE INVISIBLE RED LINE

I was born in 1965 in my parents' bed at home in England. I had a sister who was twenty-one months older than me. Later, when we moved to a small village in South Wales, my brother was born. He's nearly four years younger than me. I considered my childhood happy and normal. It was years later, in my first rehabilitation centre for alcoholism, that I was asked if I'd had a happy childhood. My immediate response was, 'Yes, very.' The therapist asked a few more questions about my parents, siblings, and early memories. I announced that my Dad was kind, loving, and never abusive. In fact, I'd considered him the fun parent. I recalled the times he would take us to the beach, and play games in the garden with us.

Family holidays were fun. We would go camping in Ireland and visit places in Europe. The drives were long, but we would play 'How many yellow/red/blue cars can you see?' or make up our own versions of what car number plates meant.

Mum, on the other hand, seemed like the strict parent—no offence intended. She had rules regarding which child did which jobs and incredibly healthy boundaries.

One of our family mottos was 'If a job's worth doing, it's worth doing properly.' Perfectly wasn't mentioned. My perfectionism and chronic people-pleasing were, unknowingly, adopted from a young age. They would become an integral reason why I never felt quite good enough, and

1

I used them in the extreme in the hope of appearing not just normal but 'perfect' in all areas of my life.

As I spilled out all this information, the therapist sat quietly, listening to every word. She then dug deeper, and it was at that moment that I realised that a lot of my childhood was an illusion created in my own mind. One thing not up for debate was the fact I knew my parents had always loved me. I don't believe parents are given an invisible handbook on how to nurture and shape their children. Yes, there are numerous books on raising children, but what is a normal childhood? I believe there is no such thing. Parents do the best they can with what they have, and they are guided by their own upbringing. I have learnt through years of therapy that our thinking, feelings, and behaviours are learnt from childhood and that they will continue on into adult life, often proving detrimental and requiring professional help.

As a child, I assumed the role of the good and perfect child (there is, of course, no such thing). I obviously wasn't good and perfect but would desperately try and keep the peace at home, by literally tap dancing (badly), playing the piano, and always being what I felt I should be at any family gathering. My Mum's parents lived nearby. Granny was wonderful. She was quite eccentric, which made her fun to be around. Grandpa, a doctor, was serious, reclusive, and stern. As children, we were scared of him. I honestly don't know why, as he never abused us or even raised his voice. It was merely his presence that made us feel as though we had to be on our best behaviour.

Dad's father sadly died when I was about four years old. My only memories of him were of him standing in front of the fire with tubes of Smarties behind his back. He would ask us to guess which hand the treat was in, and we always guessed correctly—he was a kind and lovely man. Dad's mum, I see when I look back, led a lonely life after her husband died. She was a wonderful homemaker, and we loved going there for meals. Dad was her only child, and she provided for him selflessly. I never really figured out their relationship. I know they loved each other, but the relationship seemed dutiful, and lacking communication on both sides.

I met my first best friend, who lived just up the road from me in school, around the age of eight. We would walk to school together, or sometimes Dad would drop us off there. One day she asked me to come over to play. I still remember the excitement of walking home, chanting her phone number in my head, desperately trying not to forget it. Our 'gang' then developed. There were four of us, and we went through so much together. The four of us have remained friends ever since, and they have been wonderful during my recent two years of relapsing and rehabs. I guess kids in school may have seen us as somewhat geekish. We were in neither the in crowd nor the out crowd. We were 'unique', somewhat sensible, and innocent. We went through Girl Guides and the Duke of Edinburgh's Award scheme. For our gold award, we needed to plan and map a course in the Brecon Beacons. We set off, rucksacks laden with food, a tent, and plenty of water. The weather was awful and visibility limited. Nothing could stop us. We were on our final part of achieving *gold*. The instructor had set a task that needed to be performed during our expedition; we needed to 'observe' something and give a written report. The four of us barely made it through the fog, and tensions were building. On our last day, we could barely see a hundred yards. Exhausted and pissed off with each other, we decided to write a written observation of ourselves—rather clever and a good way to solve our differences. The instructor thought it was ingenious.

In my teenage years, school took on a different meaning. Mum decided it was because I had discovered boys, which, to some extent, was true. In reality, I loved sport, played netball and hockey for the school, and learnt to play the piano.

My first alcoholic drink was a Cinzano and lemonade. I think I was about seventeen. During sixth form, my friends and I would go to the local discos and drink gin and orange, vodka and lime, or anything quite frankly. This became a regular Friday and Saturday night ritual. We drank, got drunk, and had fun.

We worked hard to save up enough money to go inter-railing around Europe. We were young and naive but full of excitement. Our month away was incredible. We camped, sleeping on beaches and even on railway platforms. One of our first campsites was in Paris. We attracted some Scandinavian men, and they joined us by our fire. We have often thought back to that night and are fairly sure we drank methylated spirits; the bottle we drank from was in a brown paper bag and had warning signs on it.

I don't remember his name, but I'll refer to him as Sven. I decided to go back to his tent. I thought we would have a kiss and fondle. Their tent was a deluxe version, with a few separate rooms. I sat in one, and 'Sven' emerged totally naked. This was not what I'd bargained for, so I scrambled out of the tent and ran back to my friends.

When we look back, we all agree how fortunate we were to have survived, given the dangerous situations we often put ourselves in. There was one night when we had eaten and drank pretty excessively and were walking back to the campsite on the edge of Lake Garda. A car pulled up alongside us. Inside were four Italian young men. One of them grabbed me and was trying to drag me into the car. One of my friends was screaming, 'Policio!'—the only word she could think of. The other started tugging at my legs, trying to pull me out of the car. Finally, I was free, lying on the side of the road, shocked and dazed. We walked back to the campsite and huddled in our tent in what we still call our 'emotional knot'. There were several other situations during which we could have been attacked or abused. But by the grace of God, we returned home in one piece and still talk about that wonderful holiday.

I had dreamed of becoming a nurse. Nursing was in the family. Both Mum and her mum had trained at University College Hospital in London, and it was advised I go there.

I went to London to train as a registered nurse. I was terrified and still remember the day Mum left me in my room in the nurses' home. It was small and dingy and overlooked some sort of furnace. The air was stale compared to the air in Wales, and as Mum left, she could hear me sobbing in my room. That must have broken her heart. It wasn't long before I threw myself into the training; true to my perfectionist nature, I did everything I was told to do.

I continued to work hard but also played hard when I could. I couldn't afford to drink. The salary was extremely low, and my money was spent on cigarettes and basic food. The only real drinking I did during my training was when we nurses got invited to the local fire or police department parties—free admission and twenty-five pence a drink, which was great. These parties didn't happen often, and shift work, plus lack of money, postponed my true alcoholism until years later. I qualified after three years of training and was a staff nurse on an orthopaedic ward for a year. I decided that nursing large people, grown-ups, was OK. But I felt compelled to move into paediatrics. I trained at Westminster Children's Hospital for eighteen months as a postgraduate student. I loved my time as a paediatric nurse. It was challenging and extremely heartbreaking at times. I witnessed horrific suffering of children and their loved ones. In those days, as a nurse, I could get into bed with the kids, read them stories, and cuddle them without being seen as a deviant.

I loved my job, did every extra course available, and made it to the position of junior sister. It was during this time that I met my first husband. It happened by chance at a mutual friend's wedding. I nearly didn't go, but my friend had mentioned a man who she thought would be perfect for me. Thankfully I went to the wedding. We clicked instantly. Life got better and better. I was falling in love with a beautiful man—a man who was caring and great fun to be with. I remember thinking, *I want to marry this man and have children with him.*

We got engaged fairly soon. My husband was working for a phone company. Mobile phones were a pretty new thing and, as many of you may remember, the size of a small brick. My husband was offered a job with a larger mobile phone company in Australia. So without any hesitation or consideration for my poor Mum and Dad, who were already arranging the wedding, we headed off on what was going to be a two-year trial in Australia. When I think back, I wonder at how utterly selfish I was. I left Mum to organise virtually everything, saying I trusted her judgement on flowers, venue, and any other decisions necessary, and left Dad to provide for it financially. I flew back six weeks before the wedding and had my dress made by a friend of a friend.

We were married in June 1992 in the village church. Before the wedding, I found myself alone with Dad for most of the morning. I was excited yet nervous, so Dad gave me a large gin and orange, which I swigged down, along with two cigarettes.

It was a wonderful day. I knew I had to behave properly, so I limited my drinking and smoking. I drank a couple of glasses of champagne at the reception and a few glasses of wine throughout the meal and speeches. The celebrations continued, with a band in the evening and an open bar. I was high on the happiness of the day and barely drank in the evening. It wasn't until we got to the hotel, where there was a complimentary bottle of champagne, that I got stuck in.

We returned to Sydney, Australia, soon after the wedding and moved into our first home. It was adorable, quaint, and overlooked bushland and sea. My husband worked hard to get this new mobile phone company up and running, and I did some nursing in one of the large hospitals. The phone business took off. Before long, it was booming, and life as corporate wife was fun, exciting, and extremely glamorous. I found myself in a world I had never known—a world of extravagant booze-filled dinners and elaborate boat cruises on Sydney Harbour.

Our first child was born in October 1993. The labour was long and hard, but when our son was finally placed on my chest, the love I felt was like nothing I had ever experienced. We took him back to the second house we lived in. He was a joy. I breastfed him on demand. He started off in his own room, but it wasn't long before he was sleeping with us. It made perfect sense; all I had to do was roll over to breastfeed him.

The joy began to fade as our son became more and more miserable. He would cry most of the time, so I would breastfeed him more and take him out in his pram, which was when he would finally sleep. I felt like a Jersey cow. My boobs were huge, and my son drained both of them within five minutes. My doctor sent me to a baby clinic I'd heard about. Its nickname was 'the place for *bad* babies'. How awful. Babies aren't born bad. I explained my son's excessive feeding to the nurse. She didn't believe he could be drinking that much, so she did a test weight. She weighed him, I fed him, and she weighed him again and was amazed at the amount he had drunk. She accused me of overindulging him and explained 'controlled crying' to me. I tried her suggestion once but couldn't bear to hear him in such distress so carried on feeding on demand. I felt envious when I met with other mothers whose babies sounded 'textbook', and I would often pretend everything was great. In truth, I was exhausted and depressed, but desperately wanted to appear like the other mothers. In order to protect my son, I will not go into detail about his condition; this story is about me. I must add, he is now over six feet tall, in good health, and highly intelligent. In fact, he's working towards his second degree in geology. His first was in maths and physics.

I remember my thirtieth birthday. My husband was away on business. His family came over for a meal and drinks and left around 9 p.m. Our son was asleep, so I danced around to 80s music and drank loads. I woke up fully dressed on the couch at 4 a.m. and stumbled into bed, only to be woken by our son two hours later.

A minister from the local church visited us one day and told me about a playgroup at the church, inviting me to come along with our son. I jumped at the idea and also started going to the Anglican church services every Sunday. Playgroup was such a relief. We both loved it. Suddenly, our son didn't seem 'different' because of his health issues, and I had people to talk to. I continued going to church, had lots of support, and ended up running the playgroup with another woman. It was wonderful. Our son loved the group and played happily with the other toddlers. I gave up my nursing career willingly once we had a child. I was privileged financially to be a stay-at-home mum, which I loved. In my mind, I decided I couldn't possibly have any more children. Our introduction to parenthood had been extremely challenging, and I worried about the risk of having another sick child.

I didn't realise I was pregnant. My husband took our son grocery shopping and came back with a pregnancy kit. I poured myself a glass of wine, peed on the stick, drank the wine, and then looked at the results in amazement—I was pregnant. My husband was thrilled. So was I, but was already worried about the baby's health. Early scans showed we were having a boy and that the hospital would have to perform periodic ultrasounds on his kidneys to determine whether he had the same condition as our son.

Somehow, by chance, it wasn't until I was thirty-six weeks pregnant that we found out we were actually having a daughter. What a wonderful surprise and, I believe, a gift from God. She was frank breech, meaning she was positioned with her bottom down, legs up, and face pointing forward. The doctor suggested a caesarean section to ensure a safe delivery. I was relieved, as the thought of delivery complications causing any health problems to our baby was terrifying.

Our son had been sleeping in our bed quite a lot. But the time came when we decided he needed to sleep in his own room. After all, we were about to have our daughter, who would be in our bed. My son loved Thomas the Tank Engine, so we bought him all Thomas bed linen, along with a small pop-up house and tried having him sleep in his own bed. He came into our room the first few nights. I explained I was getting too big and might keep him awake. He then slept in his own bed quite happily.

Our daughter was born in August 1996, happy, healthy, and an absolute joy. My husband bought our son in to meet his new sister. He was more excited about the present we'd told him she would bring. It was a Tommy train set, which he loved. I had a catheter and an IV drip. He climbed into bed with such gusto my IV nearly came out. Most of the pictures we took and sent to my family were of him, with just a few glimpses of his sister wrapped up asleep. Our son was allowed to help with her first bath. Excited and rather overzealous, he flicked the flannel and splashed the water. He was having fun, but the bath ended with his sister crying. So we thanked him very much for his help, and I finished off the bath.

I flew to Wales with both kids when our son was four and our daughter was four months old. It was the worst flight I'd ever had. I'd brought along three spare outfits for them both. Before we even took off, our daughter vomited all over herself and her brother, so one outfit down apiece already. Our son was scared of the flush in the toilets. I would go with him, his sister tucked under my arm. Those toilets are small, and it was like an endurance test to change my daughter's nappy on the flip-down shelf while her brother stood crying at the sound of the flush. I have never been more relieved to see my parents. They were waiting eagerly behind the barrier to meet their granddaughter and our son, who was now looking much fitter and healthier than he had when he was younger.

We had a wonderful Christmas. Our son loved being with his older nephew and niece, and our daughter was so easy. She would lie under the Christmas tree and play with the wrapping paper.

When we were in the middle of renovating our kitchen and our daughter was breastfeeding about five times a night, my husband was offered a job in Singapore. The four of us went out for brunch one day. Our son ordered his usual—ham-and-cheese croissant—and my husband and I ordered burgers with chips. Our daughter was on my lap breastfeeding as we ate. Suddenly, she sat up, grabbed a chip, and ate it. My husband politely said maybe it was time to reduce the breastfeeding, especially at night. I agreed. I was exhausted.

He was due to go ahead of us to Singapore, which meant I needed to juggle the renovations, along with getting the house packed up, with a four-year-old and a ten-month-old. He said he would be in charge of the controlled crying at night. Hearing her scream nearly killed me. But after four nights, she didn't feed in the night. Within two weeks, she was off the breast completely.

By this point, she was crawling. The kitchen was hazardous, and we were living with a microwave and toaster in the sitting room. I was relieved when the renovations were over, and we joined my husband in Singapore.

We stayed in a serviced apartment until we found a house in an expat community. I made sure that, wherever we lived, I took the kids to Wales every year. They adored their time there. They had a great relationship with my parents and with their cousins and adored my sister, her husband, my brother and his girlfriend, who he later married. They all visited us in Sydney, Singapore, and later America. This, coupled with our annual trips, created the incredible closeness and love we all had for each other.

I found the whole expat life shallow and not me at all. The pomp and arrogance, especially of the kids who had grown up in this environment, was appalling. We had to have a live-in maid. There wasn't another option. If you didn't have a maid, there was no chance of getting a babysitter, as the other maids weren't allowed to be 'rented out'. The maids lived in tiny box rooms off the laundry, likely the only part of the house that didn't have air conditioning, as was the case in ours. Their salaries were ridiculously low but set strictly by the government. They cooked, cleaned fanatically, washed, ironed, and got one day off a week. I didn't want someone else bringing up my children or enabling them to become spoilt brats so explained to our maid that I would only need her to babysit or care for the children if I needed to go out. She found this hard, and I would find her tidying up after our kids constantly. I had to be firm and explain why I wanted them to take some responsibility. She looked bewildered but did, in time, back off.

I remember thinking one night when we were having a dinner party, cooked and served by our maid, that the evening cost way more than what we paid her monthly. I was stuck—bound by protocol—when it came to salary. I decided the only way to make things better for her was to let her have time off when she wished, if I didn't need her.

It was during our time in Singapore I noticed my drinking change. My husband travelled a lot for work, so I found myself alone, drinking and eating crisps for dinner after the kids had gone to bed. I was only drinking a bottle of wine each night (which, by the way, was neither the drink nor the amount I ended up on by the end of my drinking career).

Our first maid **seemed nice**, but it wasn't long before she started trying to extort money from me. Her first attempt was to threaten that if I didn't give her more money, she would say that 'Sir' had made her pregnant. (The maids called us Sir and Madam, which felt extremely awkward.) I had to be firm with her, which worked for a few weeks. She then approached me again, saying if I didn't give her more money, she would hurt our kids when I was out.

My husband wouldn't be flying in until much later. Thankfully, my brother and his wife were staying with us at the time, so I didn't have to face this situation on my own. We didn't know what to do. On the advice of our neighbour, we locked the maid in her room. The following day, she was taken to what was referred to as 'the naughty maid's agency' and was deported back to her home country. We knew she had stolen CDs and had been seen flogging them in the red-light district while pushing our daughter in her buggy. But it wasn't until we got back to Sydney that we realised how many she had stolen.

I confided in my brother about my drinking. We share the same quirky sense of humour, and when I told him I was drinking a bottle of wine a night and eating a family-sized bag of kettle crisps, he laughed and said, 'At least you're getting a few of your daily servings—grapes and potatoes.' He took me to see a doctor, who suggested controlled drinking—two drinks a night and two alcohol-free days a week. Right-ho, let's give this a go. I did miraculously manage the two drinks a day but never did take a night off and would, on occasion, drink far more if my husband was home or we were with family or friends.

I made plans to take our kids to Wales. I needed a break from life. It was Chinese New Year, and business class was packed, mainly with expat families. We had two seats at the front and a fold-down cot. The kids sat in the seats, while I started putting things in the overhead locker. A small hard toy fell out and hit our daughter on the head. She began screaming, bringing on distasteful looks from passengers flying without kids. I always travelled well prepared, armed with playdough, sticker books, and snacks. The flights were hard work but worth it, as the kids were always well behaved. Our daughter was already very sociable and spent a lot of that flight talking to the hostesses. She even handed out nuts with their help. I love kids, but I drew the line at becoming the in-flight nanny. I watched parents recline, sip Champagne, and watch films as their kids 'ran amuck', and I gravitated towards my entertainment supplies. Both kids were finally asleep. I chose a film, ordered Champagne, breathed a sigh of relief, and reclined my seat. My well earned moment ended abruptly when two kids tapped me on the shoulder and asked if I wanted to play. 'Play'? Absolutely not. Their parents were asleep, so being a coward, I asked the stewardesses to sort it out, which they did.

We did get another maid after about six months. She was lovely, but I was sceptical and watched her closely. I saw her take something from the bookshelf numerous times. It turned out, she was borrowing my Bible, which I gave to her when we returned to Sydney.

Mum and Dad came to stay, and I took them to a large evangelical church I was attending. During the service, it was rather like 'spot the Anglicans'. People were waving their arms in the air. We sat with our arms firmly down! The kids loved the Sunday school, which was always full of fun activities. At Christmas, they made Nativity sets out of pegs, which they were very proud of.

We moved back to Sydney when my husband took a new job with another mobile phone company, which was based in Melbourne. This meant Monday to Friday he would be in Melbourne, and he would return home for weekends. Our son's health was stable, and I had lots of lovely friends; we would meet up regularly at beaches, playgrounds, or each other's homes. I became very involved at the Anglican church I'd previously attended—providing home-cooked meals for members in need and teaching Scripture at the local primary school once a week. My drinking was pretty average at this time, although I did drink alone when my husband was away. It was my reward after feeding the kids and getting them ready for bed.

We had talked about getting a dog and decided to wait until the kids were old enough to take some responsibility. Our new addition was a gorgeous female retriever, just a few weeks old when we got her. A tiny golden bundle of fun, who loved her new family, especially the lack of rules! Puppy training classes were attempted, but we found them to be hard work and seemingly cruel.

I have such happy memories of when the kids were younger. Unlike some of the other mums, I dreaded school holidays being over. Our home was like a resort. We had a large garden, with a cubby house and a swimming pool. This made everyday life fun, and on reflection, those years were the happiest times of my life. Call me overindulgent, which I was; I loved nothing more to create the feeling that every day was a holiday. Due to the amazing weather, the kids would rarely get dressed on weekends or school holidays. I floated around in a swimming costume and sarong, joining in the fun, and would make what our daughter called a 'posh lunch'. This consisted of a selection of sandwiches with crusts cut off, crisps, and a piece of fruit. They would spread it out on a small table in the cubby house, pull up their seats, and proceed to chat and laugh as they ate. The piece of fruit was often rolled down the slide, hidden in bushes or given to our dog!

My husband continued to climb the corporate ladder and become more and more successful. I helped out a lot at our kids' school. I would accompany them on school trips, helped out at fundraising barbecues, and spent hours in the library with other mums covering books. The latter was painful. I watched the mums with their rulers covering the books with sticky back plastic and producing perfectly 'bubble free' books. I consider myself a practical person but could not manage to cover one book without there being bubbles. Covering my kids' textbooks was no different. Their books always had loads of bubbles, sometimes huge pockets filled with air. I told my son one day how sorry I was about the way I'd covered their books and loved his response. 'Mum, I love the bubbles,' he told me. 'They give me something to play with when I'm bored in class.' It was a great lesson in not having to do things perfectly.

One time, my daughter had a school project and had to make a scene of nature that had meaning. I was never the sort of mum who would 'overly' help her kids. I believed their projects and schoolwork should be their work and knew the teachers could see where parents had helped. My daughter's scene had a green base, and we made a papier mâché volcano. We had left it to the last minute, so before it was dry, she painted it brown and green, and I put it outside to dry. To my horror, in the morning, I went to check on it and realised a possum had decided to not only nibble the top of the volcano but pee on it as well. We patched it up, she borrowed miniature animals from her brother, and we took it to school. The nature projects were all on display in the library for weeks. One day, I was in covering books, and a terrible smell filled the room. I walked over to my daughter's 'work of art' and realised it was the possum wee. We laughed about it, and thankfully, the kids took the projects home the following day.

It seemed there was always a celebration—people coming to stay, us in Wales, lunches out with girlfriends, and family barbecues. My role as a corporate wife became increasingly lavish. We hosted staff Christmas parties at our home, and dinned out in exclusive restaurants with high flying executives. Our most decadent work invite was a week on a beautiful island in the Caribbean. An exclusive, annual event for the CEOs of the different industries within the company and their partners. As a 'partner', I spent my days on speedboats, wakeboarding, being pampered with incredible beauty treatments in the spa, and drinking by the pools and on the beaches. Fridges filled with top-shelf Champagne and wine were positioned all over the island. For an alcoholic in the making, this was 'perfect'.

Despite my husband's busy work schedule, we managed to have wonderful family times. We holidayed in Bali and Fiji, as they were so close, and most summers we would rent a beach house a few hours' drive from Sydney. Always great excitement as we filled the boot and roof storage pod with food, jigsaws, board games, snorkelling gear, and boogie boards. I hang onto those precious memories. My drinking was moderate, the consequences minimal, with the occasional crippling hangover that required bacon and egg sandwiches, dozens of mugs of tea, headache pills, and an afternoon sleep if I was able.

Between the ages of 36 and 40, my drinking changed. I loved what we called 'liquid lunches' with my girlfriends. Lovely cafes on the water's edge, endless chatting, and a few large glasses of wine. All good fun—no harm done! But I remember dying to start drinking again early evening. Dinners out changed. I stopped offering to be the 'designated driver' and made the suggestion that taxis would allow for more fun. Deep down, this made me feel better. People were drinking as much as me. This was probably the first real 'drinking lie' to myself.

My kids were becoming more independent, which should have been fine—job well done! I missed the days when I was the centre of their world and how they had loved having fun with me. This, I realise, was the start of something not quite right about *me*—I loved them so much and guess

I would have liked time to stand still for a few years. I began drinking more, mainly out of boredom and lack of purpose. Of course, they still loved and needed me, but a big part of this need involved me driving them to school events and activities, plus social events with their friends. I started feeling resentful on the days I knew I'd have to drive them in the evenings. The idea of only having two drinks before the drive became an unhealthy obsession. I realised later this is at the core of addiction. I decided I'd start having a few drinks at lunchtime. 'Genius'—problem solved. The alcohol would be out of my system in time to have those two 'precious' early-evening drinks. I'm ashamed to say I sat through school plays, parent-teacher evenings, netball, and basketball games longing for them to end so I could get home and drink. I especially resented late night 'pick-ups' and thanked God for carpooling and mums who happily chose the pick-up rather than the drop-off. Here comes the denial and delusion. It never crossed my mind that 'maybe' my drinking was abnormal. My kids were extremely well cared for, the house immaculate, packed lunches prepared, meals cooked from scratch, and I was always on top of the laundry and running of the home.

Mum and Dad came to stay for my fortieth birthday. My newfound 'need' to drink at lunchtime led me to organise lunches out in lovely restaurants, which meant I could drink and not have to wait for the famous 6 p.m. opening of the Champagne. Their times with us were always wonderful. I felt safe, loved, and appreciated. I never wanted it to end.

I didn't keep tabs on when I drank or why and would find myself drinking alone most lunchtimes. Only a few glasses, but I realise now that, despite this sounding fairly innocuous, the mental obsession was there, and my 'moral compass' became challenged. On occasion, I drove knowing I was over the legal limit. This was the start of my decline into full-blown, out-of-control alcoholism. Without knowing it, I was crossing the invisible line, and there was absolutely no way back.

CHAPTER 2

DENIAL AND DELUSION

When I was forty-one, my husband took another big job, this one in New Jersey, just outside New York. So once again, we packed up and moved. We lived in a serviced apartment in New York for a while until we bought a house. My hardwired, 'unrealistic' belief that I needed to appear 'perfect' was the only reason my drinking, even though done in secret much of the time, didn't change much in the first twelve months. I made sure the relocation went smoothly, finding doctors, and dentists and getting the family settled. After all, that was my job. We moved into our house, which was lovely. But I was horrified as I watched neighbours walk to our front door bearing home-baked goods. It was just like I'd seen in films, but it was actually happening to me.

Our gorgeous golden retriever was flown out and joined us. She was so excited to see us and loved her new home. The kids thought living there was great. I was full of fear at the thought of having to socialise with these people especially as I discovered their drinking was minimal, if at all. Despite my obsessive need to drink, I did what I knew best. And in true people-pleasing fashion, I volunteered at a specialised children's hospital. I got involved with fundraising and even modelled at a charity auction event. It was funny, me modelling. I was a healthy size 12, compared to the size 2s who were also modelling. I think the event planner put me in there to inspire fuller-figured women—charming! I volunteered at my daughter's school. I worked with Spanish-speaking kids who barely spoke English. The kids loved me—no wonder, as I always arrived with a few drinks under my belt. I was fun and let them get away with things. But I did actually help them with their English language skills and literature work, which included reading and explaining Shakespeare to them. Needless to say, both voluntary jobs ended after about eighteen months. I didn't have the strength, and the paranoia about being found became too much.

My husband's younger sister and her two kids were staying when I got the phone call from Mum saying Dad had suffered a large heart attack after his scheduled hip replacement. My husband booked me on the first flight the following morning. I drank in excess, but couldn't fall asleep. I was terrified Dad would die before I got there. My sister-in-law gave me a sleeping pill, which did the trick. I slept for six hours before what seemed to be a never-ending flight. I felt physically sick as I began my drive to Wales in the hire car. I 'needed' more booze, so I stopped at one of the petrol stations and bought a few bottles of wine, one of which I drank quickly in the car before finishing the drive.

Mum and I went straight to see Dad in hospital. Seeing him hooked up to various machines and intravenous lines in his arms was terrifying. On the second day we visited, he began hallucinating. Mum got inappropriate laughter, and Dad got very cross with her. He mumbled about getting letters done for my sister's husband's business and said the sandwiches were green. Then, as the doctors approached him, he said, 'Here come the poofters.'

Suddenly, he was surrounded by doctors, nurses, and the resuscitation trolley and rushed off somewhere. The doctor explained that his kidneys were struggling along with his heart. Dad's worst nightmare came true. He was catheterised. He coped with it well and felt enormous relief as the urine poured into the catheter bag.

I visited him every day. His health improved, so I booked my flight back. Saying goodbye was one of the hardest things I've ever done. I would kiss and hug him, say goodbye, get to the door, and then run back again for more hugs. This went on for ages. In the end, he said, 'Come along now, Daught (that's what he called me). It's time to leave, or you'll miss your flight.'

So I left, praying that would not be the last time I would hug him. I drank as soon as I got in the hire car and carried on throughout my flight home.

Up until this point, my drinks of choice had been Champagne and white wine. My husband liked his variously flavoured vodkas with tonic water. He is not an alcoholic, and his ratio of vodka to tonic water was nothing like mine once I began to drink vodka. To me, America is the land of 'free pour'. I began loving vodka-based cocktails, and I reckon they contained at least three or four shots of vodka. My drinking escalated rapidly. Before long, I was drinking up to three bottles of wine a day. The volume was unbearable, so I switched to vodka. I remember someone telling me people couldn't smell vodka on your breath, which I learnt later was absolutely not true.

I remember my first morning drink vividly. The local ladies had been inviting me to join them for power walking in the mornings. I always refused. I was the 'fattest' of the lot and, in my mind, convinced it was out of sympathy. I must have been very drunk one night when I agreed, via text, to join the ladies the following morning. I woke up in my usual hung-over state and was panic-stricken when I realised what I had to do that morning. I drank numerous cups of tea and took four Ibuprofen but still felt physically sick. I had always been aware of the phrase 'hair of the dog', and this situation qualified for a 'one-off' morning drink. Two large vodkas with a splash of orange juice. My nerves had settled, and the idea of a power-walk seemed less daunting. I drank one more just to be safe, scrubbed my teeth, gargled with gallons of mouthwash, put drops into my bloodshot eyes, and had just started sucking on a mint as the walking group arrived. I have to say, I was pretty impressive. I walked fast and thought the walk had gone pretty well. But I knew I would never do it again—far too risky.

This wasn't a justified 'one-off'. It was the start of 24/7 top-up drinking. I believe I was known as what people call a functioning alcoholic—a phrase that I, quite frankly, despise. To me, it screams *denial*. And I was in it. Deluded. Vodka and I were now 'best friends'. 'Functioning'? Yes, through sheer determination to keep up appearances.

My husband snored, which gave me a great excuse to sleep in the spare room. Some nights, I would wake up and have a few swigs to get myself back to sleep. In a sick way, I thought it was funny that my husband thought I was a great morning person. I would take him a mug of tea to wake him up and prepare the children's lunchboxes, all the while topping myself up with vodka. Once my husband had left for work and the children had gone to school, I would dash around, making beds and doing the laundry, topping up all the time. Then the 'crucial' vodka check. I would drive to the supermarket to ensure the fridge was full—but, more importantly, that my vodka stash was large.

Dad's health was fragile, and he was scheduled to have a quadruple bypass and new mitral on the twenty-third of December. I flew over the day before, and my husband and kids arrived on Christmas Eve. The operation took twelve hours. We all did our own thing. Mum and my brother took themselves off on separate walks. My sister went home, and I sat in Dad's office crying and drinking.

We visited him early evening. We were only allowed in two at a time, so Mum and my sister went first and then me and my brother. Despite the huge amounts of alcohol I'd drunk, I felt suddenly sober, and the pain was all consuming. I held Dad's hand and talked to him, praying he could hear me. We then sat in a small room, and Mum prayed for Dad and us.

Mum visited Dad early on Christmas day and then joined us in church. She managed to produce the lunch. It was exactly as it had always been, delicious, but there was no Dad at the table. The way Mum said grace made me realise she was being totally 'carried' by God. That lunch, other meals, and the way she held the family together could only have come from him. We all visited him later that day. My husband and kids had never seen so many machines and were devastated. They absolutely adored my Dad. He always gave us small funny presents on Boxing Day, joke gifts like bandaged fingers with fake blood and a nail sticking through it or miniature set of playing cards. Despite being so frail, he'd managed to buy the presents before he went into hospital, and it was my job to hand them out.

We flew back before Dad was out of hospital, which was heart-wrenching. Again, I remember praying this wouldn't be the last time we saw him.

Back to my 'imprisoned' miserable life, which was now one big lie to myself and loved ones. When my husband wasn't travelling, I would do my usual top-up drinking throughout the day and greet him with a glass of Champagne in hand, saying I'd opened the bar early. I would pass out every night on the couch while watching TV and rationalise it by saying what a hectic day I'd had, volunteering or organising fundraising events. I resented my husband when he worked from home. How was I supposed to drink in my usual way? I would tell him I was heading off to the gym, meeting friends, volunteering, or having a shopping day in NYC. My truth included driving to shopping malls and finding the most secluded spot, usually in the basement. The excitement factor was huge; in fact, the planning, buying, and hiding of it was often better than drinking it. Still believing I was 'fine', once parked, I'd drink excessively and sing along to 80s music. This 'happy time' lasted about half an hour. I would then climb onto the back seats and sleep before heading home. In fact, everybody/ thing was an inconvenience, even our lovely cleaning lady who came once a week. I would often say I had a migraine and head off to bed, asking her to clean the spare bedroom last. I was incapable of doing anything without drink. So the 'game' of me, myself, and I evolved. I was now drinking a bottle of vodka a day, and more some days, depending on the ease in which I could 'get away with it'.

I had vodka stashed all over the house, inside long boots, up sleeves of jackets, and in coloured drink bottles at the back of the cupboard under the kitchen sink behind all the cleaning products. And I made sure I never ran out. I started to forget what my children had said the night before or if I'd even kissed them goodnight. I would casually chat with them while they were eating breakfast and ask them to remind me if there were any after-school activities that day. Our daughter was very sporty. She played soccer well, which meant weekly training and matches.

I remember one of her matches with absolute disgust. The mums were all in their fold-out chairs, me included. Our daughter came over at halftime and said she had forgotten her water bottle. She wanted to know if she could borrow mine. Oh shit! My bottle was virtually neat vodka, so I quickly said I had a sore throat and didn't want her to catch it. I then drove to the nearest shop and bought her a new bottle.

During our time in America, I regularly went to an Evangelical church. I loved the services but had already consumed between three to four large vodkas before I went. I would sing and clap and never once worried that anyone would smell the vodka on me. After all, in my deluded mind, I was having a jolly good time. I felt chuffed about being there, it was one of the few remaining ploys to attempt to keep up appearances.

19

My days went something like this—drink, tidy the house, drink, plan the evening meal, drink, lock the doors, and pass out on the couch with the alarm on my phone set for half an hour before the children were due back from school. I would leap up, brush my teeth, spray myself with perfume, and always ensure I had a mint or chewing gum in my mouth when they arrived home. They loved having friends over to play. We had a huge basement with a pool table, a large TV, an Xbox, and all 'trimmings'. The setup was handy for me; the kids were in the basement as I carried on drinking. I would order pizza in. That kept them happy and still in the basement.

My husband was convinced I was depressed, so I went to a psychiatrist. He was a lovely man who asked me nothing about my drinking. No offence to American doctors, but in my opinion, they are very drug happy. I left with a prescription for antidepressants, Xanax, and an anti-anxiety drug. I didn't bother taking any of them, as alcohol was my cure for everything.

I was getting stomach problems so I was referred to a gastroenterologist, who decided to perform an endoscopy and colonoscopy. The instructions about what to eat and drink for a week before the surgery were easy. I was barely eating. The night before the surgery, I had to consume a huge quantity of bowel-cleansing liquid and knew I would be on the toilet for hours. I explained to the family that I would be in my room most of the night. I drank the prep fluid slowly and remembered the doctor saying clear fluids only. *Marvellous!* Vodka is clear. So that was my evening—drunk and on the toilet for about four hours.

As a family, we flew to Wales for Dad's seventieth birthday. He was a big kid at heart and decided it would be an optional fancy dress party based on Desperate Dan and *The Beano* comic. My husband and son hired Lord Snooty outfits, which were brilliant, including even a top hat and black cane. Our daughter and I shopped around and went as Minnie the Minx. So did Mum. The party was so much fun, with wonderful speeches. I tried hard to limit my drinking, in honour of Dad, but I was swigging vodka from bottles hidden in my wardrobe.

My Dad's mum was in a nursing home and very close to death. We visited her. She was like a tiny bird, all her limbs cramped up, but was being kept pain-free.

We flew back to America the following day. Two days later, my Mum rang to say Dad's mum had died. So back I went, alone this time. I drank the entire flight and during the drive down to Wales and arrived looking and feeling awful. Dad's mum only had a few friends, and her last ten years had been spent in various nursing homes. I'm sure my family wondered why I cried so much at the funeral. I hadn't particularly liked her. I know it was the booze that made me cry. I was 'dying' inside, and it was a chance to let out my desperation. The funeral was small, and to me, it signified what a sad and lonely life she'd had. My other Granny, who I adored, had died some year previously. Their lives couldn't have been more different. This showed at their funerals. There was standing room only at Granny's and a true celebration of her life and wonderful qualities. My trips to Wales were becoming increasingly challenging, with my need to be permanently topped up. The morning after the funeral, I had showered, swigged more vodka, dried my hair, brushed my teeth, and sprayed perfume. When I walked out of my bedroom, which was next to Dad's office, he said, 'Interesting smells, Daught.' I don't think he meant the perfume, but he didn't challenge me. From the outside, we looked like the perfect family— the very successful husband, the great corporate wife and devoted loving mother, and the two beautiful kids. But I was miserable inside. The only time I felt OK was when I drank.

In spite of my drinking, we had some wonderful family holidays during our time there. The kids' favourite was the holiday in the RV. The night before we left, I was drunk as usual. I had given my entire body a fake tan, and I was ready for the trip. Then I fell asleep in the spare bedroom. I awoke in the morning, having not washed the gel off the night before. Not only was I seriously hung over, but I had an extremely dark, patchy tan. We flew to Vegas and booked into a beautiful hotel. My fear was already there. How could I possibly not only buy but also hide the vodka in an RV? It was about forty degrees when we picked up our RV. There was a hold-up, so I volunteered to go and get basic groceries. Of course, I needed to get enough booze to see me through the trip.

The RV was a huge white thing with 'Cruise America' written in bold lettering along both sides, accompanied by a picture of the perfect happy family. My husband had planned the trip, including where we would go, and he'd booked us into RV sites for every night. Thankfully, my husband liked to drink, so there was always wine around. But I was forced to reduce my alcohol consumption quite dramatically during the holiday.

My husband's planning went somewhat haywire on a few occasions. One night, we arrived in our huge vehicle at what we thought was going to be a lovely RV site. Instead, we arrived at a trailer park in the middle of nowhere. When we pulled into the site, all we saw were old small mobile homes without wheels or cars that were occupied. In true positive spirit, we hooked up to the power and sewage line and decided to explore the grounds. Well, that took all of five minutes. There was a small pool that stunk of chlorine and had unknown foreign objects, including what looked like balls of human hair, along the bottom. It was so hot the kids wanted a swim. Of course, I let them get in, but I refused to get in myself.

We had a wonderful time and saw amazing natural beauty. To this day, our kids say it was their favourite holiday. If only I could have cherished the fact. I'd loved our time away, despite drinking significantly less. I was 'present', participating, laughing loads, able to function well, and 'remembered' everything. Fact is, I went straight back to 24/7 alcoholic misery, which was going to get unbelievably worse.

We also took a short trip to Canada, where we stayed in a lovely hotel and did the whole Niagara Falls thing. It was incredible, but yet again I was top-up drinking, and the 'cheesy' superimposed photo of us in ponchos beneath the falls said it all. My face was red and bloated, my eyes vacant.

My husband, thinking my 'depression' was worsening, generously booked me into a lovely boutique hotel in downtown Manhattan for a weekend. I can't begin to tell you the excitement I felt—a weekend of drinking as much as I liked. A driver picked me up at lunchtime on the Friday and drove me to the hotel. I was greeted with Champagne on arrival and then whisked myself off to my room, armed with a small case containing three bottles of expensive Champagne and my sexiest clothes. I drank the first two bottles in my room and then fell asleep for four hours. Time to start the last bottle, as I prepared for the evening. I showered, had my hair and makeup done, and then headed to the bar. I felt fabulous, sitting casually on a bar stool, ordering a cocktail that an older man sitting next to me paid for. This was very new; I'd never sat in a bar alone. Within minutes my glass was empty. He ordered another and proceeded to ask far too many questions, so I excused myself by saying I needed the bathroom. I had been flattered, but alcoholic grandeur set in and 'I knew' I could spend my time with someone much younger and far more attractive. Within seconds I had another man buying me a drink. This was becoming fun. Feeling exhilarated and pretty sexy, I began imagining the possibility of having a 'one-night stand'. Really! I'd never cheated on my husband and had zero tolerance for infidelity. But if I was going to do it, why not make it count and aim for someone gorgeous?

There was a group of young men in the corner, one of whom kept staring at me. He finally came over and asked if I was OK. He had been watching me and wondered why I was alone, so he sat next to me and ordered us drinks. I poured out all sorts of lies about my husband. He listened as he moved his stool nearer.

It must have been around 2 a.m. that we staggered up to my room, kissing passionately in the elevator and finally getting the key card to work. I don't remember all of the details. All I know is that I woke up in the morning wearing nothing but a pair of thigh-high suede boots, and the room looked chaotic. I slipped out of bed and went straight to the bathroom, where I redid my hair and face. But I couldn't bend down to remove the boots for fear of throwing up. I slipped back into bed and looked across at this twenty-nine-year-old Adonis. He woke up, smiled, and asked, 'What next?' I suggested a Champagne breakfast in bed. *I needed a drink.* We remained in bed for most of the day, ordering more Champagne and a light lunch. I never got his name. Feeling no remorse, I returned home the next day.

My drinking was affecting my health. I had constant diarrhoea, and I barely ate. Morning drinking had become a major battle. The first drink, and often the second and third, came straight up. Desperate for the effect, I carried on until it stayed down. I was now suffering excruciating heartburn, so I was referred back to my gastroenterologist. He booked me in for an endoscopy. It was done on a Friday morning, and I drank before the procedure, as usual. The exam located some damage to my stomach lining, which had been caused by the vodka—not that I admitted that—and I was put on a drug to help with my gastric reflux. I was also instructed not to drink any alcohol that day, which of course I did.

The company my husband was working for was sponsoring a famous female singers USA tour, and the opening night was that night. Our daughter was so excited about the event. I moderated my drinking quite well that afternoon, for fear of not looking like my usual 'perfect corporate wife' self. The three of us were picked up by a driver and dropped off, and we headed to the VIP area. My husband knew I shouldn't be drinking after the endoscopy, but I sipped a glass of Champagne gracefully. Two more followed, and all I remember was 'coming to' on a large red couch in the shape of giant lips. I was then taken off in a wheelchair and driven to Newark Hospital, which was in a rough area and packed, given it was a Friday night. I waited on a trolley next to the nurses' station for a few hours and then asked my husband if we could go home. We did. I had no thought about our daughter. Thankfully, she was with my husband's PA and her teenage daughter, and she kindly dropped her home later. I woke up the following morning crippled with guilt and shame about our beautiful daughter and then proceeded to drink as usual.

My stash had run out, which rarely happened, so I drank one of my husband's flavoured bottles of vodka. I replaced it, but he said it was strange that the bottle of Citron was gone and a different flavour was in its place. I said I had no idea what had happened to it and that I hated the taste of vodka unless it was in a cocktail.

Our kids went on Camp America trips a few times while we were there. My husband and I had a breakaway, driving up the East Coast. It was stunning, but again I was faced with the fear of not being able to get enough booze. We arrived at a beautiful resort, unpacked, and went exploring. My husband needed the break. He worked very hard and was happy to lay by the pool. That was perfect. I went back to our room and drank every miniature white spirit there was. Before dinner, my husband fancied a vodka tonic. He was horrified when he tasted it. I had filled the bottles up with water. He rang reception, and the hotel was very obliging and replaced the bottles. My husband said to me, 'Who on earth would do something like that? This isn't a cheap place. They must have enough money.' I agreed wholeheartedly.

I was due to fly to Wales one night for a 'break'. But instead of packing, I drank in my usual way—drink, pass out, drink, pass out. I came to at about twelve o'clock and looked around. The house was a mess, there was barely any food in the fridge, the laundry pile was enormous, and I was incapable of doing anything about it. So I drank some more. It was at that moment I remembered all the pills I had in our bathroom. *This is it*, I told myself. *Time for me to leave this world.* I've heard it said 'People who talk about committing suicide are far less likely to follow through than those who stay silent.' This was true for me. Rather than being honest about my drinking and reaching out for help, I made the drunken, catastrophic decision to end my life. It seemed a far more appealing way to end this living hell than admit to the life of lies in which I was drowning. At the time, I was incapable of comprehending the devastating, life-ruining effect it would have had on my loved ones, especially my kids. I drank some more and then took a huge amount of Xanax.

I have no idea how many of the pills I took, but as I lay on the bed, I started losing feeling in my legs. I panicked and thought, *I have to make myself sick.* But it was too late. My body was now limp. One of the sickest and most devastating texts my husband received was the one I sent him before I passed out. It simply read, 'I'm sorry. Please tell the kids I love them.'

Our house was about to be put on the market for sale, as we had decided to move back to Australia so that our son could do his final two years of school there. I believe what happened next was an act of God. The real estate agent who was selling our home dropped in a day early to see if I needed a hand staging the house for the viewings. She heard my mobile phone ringing upstairs and found me unconscious. She must have answered it and told my husband what had happened.

His drive home was at best forty minutes. I can't imagine the panic and fear he was experiencing. I was put in an ambulance and taken to the nearest hospital. My husband had missed the ambulance, and upon arriving at home, all he saw was yellow crime tape around the house.

I don't remember anything of the few days that followed. When I finally woke up, I was in a single room. I was still hooked up to IVs and a catheter, and I saw a large Jamaican woman sitting on a chair by the door. My first thoughts were unbelievable shame and then fear that my truth was out, with the initial blood test showing a dangerously high level of alcohol as well as benzodiazepines. The next thought was, *How the hell can I get out of here? I* need *a drink.* Now, if that's not addiction and insanity at its worst, I have no idea what is.

My husband arrived, and a psychiatrist joined us. She explained that my suicide attempt meant I had been 'sectioned' under the Mental Health

Act and would spend a week in a secure locked unit. I sobbed and pleaded for her to let me go home. My husband vouched that he would care for me and not leave my side, but the law was the law.

I remember being wheeled into the unit, in absolute disbelief that I'd ended up in a mental institution. My husband dropped off clothes, toiletries, and so on, which were all checked by the staff. My toiletries were locked away and handed back twice a day under staff supervision, and the cords that held my pyjamas up were cut off. I was shown to my room. It had two beds in there, but the second was free thankfully. Feeling terrified and unsafe, I went to the nurses, who were behind reinforced Perspex, and poured out my fears. They assured me that I would be safe.

In the middle of the night, one of the patients, a large man, came charging into my room banging a laundry trolley against my bed. I was petrified. In less than a minute, he was removed by two security guards, sedated, and put in a room that was padded from floor to ceiling. In the morning, the staff moved me into a shared room with an older woman. My new roommate seemed pleasant, if rather eccentric. But I would soon discover that she simply wandered around totally naked talking nonsense. My first night and subsequent nights in with her were awful. She would try and climb into bed with me and was convinced I was her daughter.

I thank God for humour. It is something I've always loved and found wonderfully mood altering. I'm not saying my situation was in any way funny—it was the most selfish act I'd ever performed—but on the humorous side, I found some of the measures put in place to ensure our safety quite hilarious. The showers had a red cord to pull in case of emergencies. It was so short I could barely reach it, and I'm five foot seven. The blood pressure machine, with its long cords, was always out, and I often sat, chuckling inside, imagining I had a lead role in *One Flew Over the Cuckoo's Nest* as we sat, lined up in hard-back chairs staring at a tiny TV.

We had daily schedules. Morning therapy was always interesting. We sat in a circle and 'talked about our feelings'. If you didn't attend this group, your punishment was exclusion from afternoon art. I found these morning sessions quite entertaining and spent them looking around and thinking how sick these people were. The truth was, I was just as sick but in denial. There was a young girl who spent the entire session pulling out strands of her hair and then sucking on the roots. Not much was said by anyone. There was the occasional psychotic outburst, and the patient would be removed. Art was my favourite time of the day. I painted wooden pots, one of which I gave to our beautiful daughter, and threading beads on elastic was appealing.

I saw my allocated psychiatrist three times and gave him some ridiculous excuses, among them, 'I was having a bad day.' When he suggested I might be an alcoholic, I was outraged. The next suggestion was easier to entertain. 'Maybe you're a functioning alcoholic?'

He was right, but I told myself I could stop if I really wanted to. I was 'functioning', and things looked good from the outside. But there was nothing functional about needing vodka to start my day or, for that matter, to do anything.

I met a fellow alcoholic in the ward who had tried to hang himself. We stuck together like glue amid the chaos. We exchanged numbers and said we would keep in touch.

One evening, there was an announcement made over the loudspeaker requesting the two of us to go to a certain room and attend an AA meeting. I knew virtually nothing about AA, but the word *anonymous* ran through my head. I jumped up, banged on the thick Perspex screen, and shouted, 'How dare you call us by name? It's supposed to be anonymous.'

A nurse calmly said, 'Look around. Do you actually think the other patients heard or even understood what was said?'

Fair call, so we went into a small room and sat with three large men. I was still outraged and in total denial about my drinking, so I heard nothing other than a phrase I will never forget: 'This disease stretches from Park Lane to park bench.' It was years later I actually realised how true that was.

My husband had lied for me and told our kids and my family that I was in for depression. The lie was kind, but the truth came out later and naturally devastated my kids and family.

I was discharged home and ordered to attend a day programme, where I would randomly be breathalysed. Thankfully, I was never selected, and in true 'perfectionist style', I completed the time. What a relief.

My drinking continued. By this point, I was drinking up to a bottle and a half of vodka a day. I remembered the man I'd met in the locked ward. I was drinking in my usual way and decided to text him and ask him over 'for a cup of tea'.

He arrived a few days later at around 9 a.m. My husband was away with work, our kids were in school, and the two of us were alone. Naturally, no tea was involved. We drank excessively and laughed about our time 'locked up'. We spent most of the day in bed, only getting up to drink more. I remember lying in bed hearing the Mexican gardeners blow the autumn leaves away. I had lost all sense of pride. What if someone had decided to pop in or the kids had come home early from school?

I will now disclose the humiliation of 'alcoholic diarrhoea,' a detail I had thought I would take to my grave. As my alcoholism progressed, so did my sense of 'urgency'. I was barely eating, so all that ever came out was liquid. It had snowed heavily one night. The following morning, I decided to brave the snow with our dog, and I'd barely made it a hundred yards before I felt that awful sense of urgency. I walked slowly in a style I like to call the penguin walk—buttocks clenched and knees together.

I was nearly at the house when it happened. I could feel the warm diarrhoea oozing down my legs so walked quickly back to the house. Once inside, any 'normal' person who had accidentally shit herself would head straight to the shower. Not me. I shuffled upstairs and downed a huge vodka to get over what had happened. I showered and carried on drinking. Why shouldn't I? This had been a terrible experience.

Needless to say, I was caught short on a few other occasions, but I did not stop drinking. I was willing to live with the problems alcohol was now causing. I have always been a girly girl. I love trips to the beauty salon for pampering and getting my hair and nails done. Somehow, through my madness, I only missed one hair appointment. Looking good for what? I barely went out. Nearly all my drinking was behind closed doors.

We were fortunate to be living in the United States of America and witnessing Obama being voted in as the first black president. Schools were shut on the day it was announced. My son was out with friends. I was with my daughter, and a lovely black plumber had come to fix our boiler. The TV was on. The counting of the votes was coming to an end. I was drunk but suddenly thought about the plumber. I invited him to join us as we watched this momentous occasion and offered him a drink. He looked puzzled and politely asked for just a glass of water. Why would I possibly think he would like a double vodka tonic?

I drove to a large outlet store, an hour's drive away. I did some shopping and then went to find my car. I spent an hour pressing the car flicker on different levels of the car park. I was sure I'd parked on level 3. I finally remembered I had both sets of car keys and had driven my husband's car, which was why I couldn't find mine. I eventually did find his car. 'Park lane to park bench' rang in my head as I crawled onto the back seats of the Mercedes, fell asleep, and then drove home—all the while still thinking what I was doing was perfectly OK.

Towards the end of our time in America, our gorgeous dog was diagnosed with cancer in her hip. We had thought what was ailing her was arthritis and were devastated to hear the news. The vet gave us options of amputation of the hip and leg and 'doggy psychotherapy'. The latter I personally found quite ridiculous. I believed all she needed was to be loved and to be free of pain. One morning after our walk together, she became irritable and aggressive and bit me on the arm. I rang the vet, who suggested that the cancer may have spread to her brain. It would be kinder and safer if she was put down sooner rather than later he told me.

It was a heartbreaking decision, but we arranged the day. Naturally, this was 'all about me'. I drank loads that day, and we all took her to the vet. As the mum, I should have been there supporting my kids. Instead, I was far more dramatic and cried more than anyone else—no support whatsoever.

The time had come for us to move back to Australia, and in my mind, I honestly believed I would be able to cut right back and drink, as I had in my mid-thirties. Needless to say, we moved back, and my alcoholism came with me. I didn't cut down and justified it by thinking how lovely it was to be back and celebrating with my lovely friends, whom I'd missed so much. We had rented out our house while we were away so moved into a rental house for just over a month while our things were shipped. Both kids went back to their old school. After a few weeks, our son announced he wanted to enrol in a new school in which he could do the international baccalaureate programme. This would give him a better chance of going to college in America. We looked into it, and the fees were outrageously high, so we managed to convince him to study in the United Kingdom.

29

On the day we moved back into our house, my husband and a girlfriend were in the house receiving all our stuff. My job was to clean the rental house. I tried so hard, but the more I drank, the harder it became. I would sleep for an hour and then try again. My husband couldn't understand why it was taking me so long. I knew why but couldn't possibly say. I want to say here that every waking minute was taken up with planning to get the booze, drinking it, and disposing of the empties. It was mentally exhausting, and the fear was crippling—though obviously not crippling enough to make me stop. Meanwhile, I still believed I could stop if I really wanted—*bullshit.*

CHAPTER 3

I KNOW, I KNOW, I KNOW BEST ...

It was not by choice that I made an appointment with my GP. My husband could see how sick I was. I believe that, deep down, he knew I was an alcoholic. I had known my GP since our son was born. She was excellent at her job. So when I walked into her room, it was no wonder that she looked at me in horror. I was bloated by alcohol, my skin was blotchy, and my eyes were bloodshot. She asked me how much I was drinking. Naturally, I lied, but she ordered blood tests anyway.

When I returned to get the results, my husband was with me. My GP looked puzzled at what the tests had revealed, given the quantities of alcohol I had said I was consuming. My liver enzymes were seriously raised. We chatted, and I agreed to cut down. She gave me a leaflet on using self-evaluation to determine whether you were drinking too much. I went through it slowly, putting ticks alongside the items that applied to me. I'd ticked every box. Time to do this 'properly', so I removed some of the ticks. (Has your work suffered as a result of your drinking? Has it led to financial insecurity? Have loved one's expressed concern? Do you wake up shaking?) Great! I wasn't actually an alcoholic. The leaflet had clarified that.

What happened next is all a bit of a blur. I ended up, reluctantly, in my first rehab, courtesy of my husband. I arrived drunk and obnoxious. I answered questions to determine my state of mind. Who was the prime minister? Obama, of course! What was the weather like? Who gives a shit! I'd blown a 3.5 on the breathalyser, seven times over the legal limit, and had to wait for it to come down to 1 before detox could begin. An agonising six hours, drinking gallons of water, vomiting, and experiencing true withdrawal for the first time. Again my husband kindly agreed to tell the kids, along with my friends and family, that I was at the clinic for depression. This was a hat I would far rather wear than one of an alcoholic.

It was a three-week programme. I lasted one week and then talked my way out of there, thinking surely I could cut down for the sake of my marriage and my kids. But as addicts know, my desire to change would not be sufficient. Within days, I was once again drinking up to a bottle and a half of vodka a day. I was put back into the same rehab three weeks after my first stay. This time, my husband couldn't lie for me. It was tearing him apart. He took it upon himself to inform my family and all my friends that I was at the centre for treatment of alcoholism. I remember sobbing under my sheets, sweating and shaking as I detoxed, and unspeakably distraught that my secret was out. In hindsight, it was a relief, as the shame of having to tell everyone myself could have pushed me over the edge emotionally.

I stayed the full three weeks and attended all the groups. Part of my stay involved going to six AA meetings a week. We were taken in a minibus, and quite frankly, I hated every meeting. Someone at every meeting always said, 'Listen to the similarities, not the differences.' I did no such thing. I have to be honest about my approach to the stories others were sharing. Rather than seeing similarities between their stories and mine, I would sit there feeling sorry for these people in so-called recovery. They had done shocking, disgusting things while drunk. I, on the other hand, believed I hadn't done much wrong at all, apart from maybe not being present for my kids. I hadn't smacked them, they were fed and dressed well, and the home was always in order. I heard about the 'yets', things that could happen to me if I continued to drink, which included being arrested for drunk driving, losing custody of my kids, and seeing my husband leave me. Surely not—these were things that happened to 'real' alcoholics!

I was under the care of a wonderful psychiatrist, a woman who was very wise but firm. Every Friday morning, she led a compulsory meditation group. She would start by going around the room and asking us what our choice of *poison* was. It was years later that I understood what she meant. Alcohol is, without doubt, poison to me.

During that stay, my husband came to visit me with the kids. It was wonderful to see them. They looked remarkably happy and excited. They had been looking at golden retrievers on a dog rescue site and had found an adorable male retriever. They wanted my approval, which of course I gave.

He had been abused, and the woman who ran the rescue centre told them they would have to leave him to his own devices until he felt safe with them. This was hard, especially for the kids, who wanted to cuddle, love, and play with him. When I arrived home, there he was at the bottom of the stairs, ears hung low. In my mind, he didn't like me, which was nonsense. That dog became a big reason to get up in the morning. He always greeted me with tail wagging, hungry, and ready for his walk.

My husband nicknamed me the 'Rehab Queen', which was fitting. It would become even more so further down the track. I had come to enjoy rehab in a sick way. It was safe, and I loved the sense of belonging and the laughs we shared during free time. I would sit with the other clients in the garden, and we would exchange funny stories about where we'd hidden our stash and the things we'd got away with. None of it was funny at all in hindsight. In truth, these discussions gave people, myself included, new ideas.

The funniest story I heard was from an older American woman. I met her just before she was due to leave. She looked immaculate—twin set and pearls kind of lady. She told us her favourite hiding place for a bottle of vodka was inside a turkey in the freezer. Ingenious, I laughed and still do at the thought of this sweet old lady swigging from a turkey's bum!

On a serious note, I look back now and feel exhausted when I think of my drinking. It was all a frenetic, draining, continuously looping mess. And all the while, I still believed I was fine. That word—*fine*—was described to me by a therapist in rehab as meaning, 'fucked up, insecure, neurotic, and emotional'. That was me.

I left that rehab with a sense of hope and determination. I had hated the AA meetings we were taken to in rehab, and was quite sure they wouldn't benefit me in any way. I lied constantly, saying I was going to AA meetings in the evening when, in fact, I would park the car at the end of a nearby street, sneak back to the garage store room, make myself a comfy 'den' out of sleeping bags, drink, fall asleep, and then wake up when my phone alarm went off. I would then put eye drops in, put a mint in my mouth, drive my car back into the garage, and then walk into the house, saying it had been a great meeting. And I was off to bed. Truth was, I didn't want my family to see or smell me. There was the notorious 'sniff test' my husband would do. This involved getting close and kissing me. I would hold my breath and pray he couldn't smell the vodka.

I don't know why I was surprised to find out my husband knew full well I was drinking. He arranged for me to go back to rehab. I remember waking up the morning I was due to go in. I drank any vodka I could find. When my husband announced he was taking our new dog out for a walk, I had an hour to pack. I'd finished the vodka, and I was desperate. Thankfully, I found a bottle of red wine (belonging to my husband—I'd never drunk red wine). I hated the taste, but in desperation, I downed the bottle, holding my nose. Needless to say, my packing was chaotic, and my husband was not impressed.

So back I went for my third admission. This time, my husband didn't even get out of the car. He popped the boot, and I got my case and staggered in drunk again. The staff were lovely. And I went through the now-familiar routine of detoxing, followed by attending groups and AA meeting.

The psychiatrist who I'd met during my previous stay was very firm with me and accused me of not taking this seriously. I hadn't. But this time, I felt so desperate I was finally open to anything. At one of the AA meetings I attended, an older woman shared her story. I listened in amazement as she gave a powerful, honest share that ended full of hope. I asked her to be my sponsor, and she agreed.

Before I left rehab, I agreed to go on a drug called Antabuse. If you drink while taking this medication, you will become seriously ill and may even die. When I left rehab, I started going to AA meetings. Quite honestly, I was doing it to show my husband and sponsor I was serious. In fact, the only reason I wanted sobriety was to save my marriage and become a good mum again. I wasn't doing it for myself, which I would come to understand years later was the key. I had to do it for myself first. If I did, then everything else would fall into place.

I worked closely with my sponsor, attended three or four AA meetings a week, and had a very poor attempt at achieving the first three of the twelve steps. I stopped taking the Antabuse when I was thirty days sober, managed to get ninety days of sobriety under my belt, and was given a precious chip. The following day, the madness set in. I felt so proud of myself I thought I deserved to celebrate with a drink. I got very drunk.

My husband came home from work and looked devastated. He took me to an AA meeting, and I sat humiliated between him and my sponsor. I had to stand up and admit what I had done to people who had cheered and clapped for me the day before to celebrate my sobriety. I suffered awful 'drinking dreams' during the first few months of sobriety. They were incredibly vivid. I would wake up drenched in sweat, convinced I'd had a drink. I had to get up, go downstairs, and have a mug of tea, and it could take up to ten minutes to realise it was only a dream. The *relief* was amazing.

So, back to step one. We admitted we were powerless over alcohol, that our lives had become unmanageable. I disliked being told I was back at the beginning and argued with my sponsor that I had already 'got' the first three steps and it was time to move onto step four. Having such a strong sense of being 'right' led me to look for a new sponsor who would understand me—after all, I was still 'different'. The search didn't happen. I decided I could take myself through the steps quite easily. My arrogance and delusion didn't lead to picking up a drink. It alienated me from AA, which was a necessary, God-given part of recovery, and kept me stuck in perpetual anxiety and fear.

Thankfully the emotional pain far surpassed my need to be right, and I found myself being honest for the first time in AA and found a new sponsor. I grew to like AA. I hadn't been put off by the calico banners that mentioned the word *God*, as I was a Christian. I was attending the Anglican church I'd been a part of years previously. I later decided to move to a Baptist Church, which was walking distance from our home, and I joined a small group of ladies for weekly Bible study. This was to become, my 'spiritual home', a place of love, understanding, and support.

My life started to improve. The kids were happy, and I was meeting up with my lovely friends for walks, coffees, and lunches. Deep down, though, I still felt consumed with shame and fear that I would drink again. I had already robbed myself of enough of life, including my kids' lives. A lot of my energy was taken up 'white knuckling', as they say in AA. This was hanging on for dear life, using my own sheer determination and self-will. No time to stop, pause, and do the AA suggested things, which were in fact quite simple. I heard it said 'it's a simple program for complicated people'. Spot on. My new sober life revolved around desperately trying to put things right with my husband and kids, and my thought process was in constant overdrive.

'Sorry' had become one of my most-used words, which I now realise is such an empty word when used in the context of my relapses and all-consuming shame. Actions really do speak louder than words, as I was to find out the hard way. AA talks about 'living amends', which is something I didn't grasp for several months. The concept is simple, effective, and crucial in early recovery. For my husband and kids, all they wanted was to see me sober and have their wife/ mum back. 'Self will run riot' was another AA gem, which proved to be my biggest barrier to emotional sobriety. My son rarely swore, but on one of the many occasions when I would follow both kids around saying sorry, he turned to me and said, 'Stop saying sorry and just don't fucking drink.'

I liked the 'war stories' in AA, but I was still not doing the suggested thing of listening to the similarities, not the differences. I heard people talk about how they had stolen, beaten their wives while blacked out, and done time in prison. *This is not my story*, I thought. All I wanted to hear was another alcoholic mum talk about her despair, and I longed for the day a woman would share about her experience of alcoholic diarrhoea.

That day finally came. I was so relieved, and after the meeting, I thanked the woman who'd bravely shared. The phrase 'Addiction stretches from Park Lane to park bench' was becoming more real, as I sat in meetings with doctors and lawyers, mums and dads, internationally known celebrities, people with chronic mental health problems, and homeless people. The list could go on. I enjoyed the sense of belonging in meetings, and as time passed, I began to realise I was no different to these people I'd previously judged. I definitely qualified and had earned my seat in the rooms.

The first time I heard alcoholism described as cunning, baffling, and powerful, placing a stranglehold on the alcoholic's recognition of the disease, I shrugged it off. I was full of ego and boosted by a mind that told me I was a survivor and could beat this if I really wanted to. The notion is laughable now, to me and to anyone reading this who is in recovery. I cannot stay sober and be of sound mind unless I do *all* the suggested things and make recovery the most important thing in my life. Without that, I'll be a hopeless case, go insane, and very possibly attempt suicide (and do it properly this time). That is the absolute *truth*.

Even though I wasn't drinking, my thinking could be way off at times. I now know that during this recovery, a lot of my thinking and behaviours were that of a 'dry drunk'. I thrived on chaos, ran on self-will, and honestly believed that as long as I wasn't drinking, everything was *fine*. 'Washing machine head' and 'stinking thinking', more AA realities, were often in play.

As the months went by, my destructive thinking and behaviours slowly began to shift, thanks to AA and its members. I felt disheartened in the early days, when I heard members say, 'We were sick for a long time, so I'll take a long time to get well.' My natural response was 'I want to fix this *now*, or as quickly as possible.' Patience is a virtue and not one that has come easily to me throughout my life.

There were many times when it all felt too hard. So many of my core beliefs needed to change. I would find myself curled up on the couch sobbing and feel this 'recovery' journey was not something I could grasp fully, let alone maintain. My second sponsor was brilliant and helped me so much. I worked through the twelve steps twice, and did numerous 'mini' step fives with her. I endured some devastating and soul-destroying things during this recovery, and I needed to work through them to remain sober and regain hope and gratitude.

I needed routine, which evolved quite quickly. Four days a week, I went to yoga classes, I met up with girlfriends for coffees and lunches, and I loved my walks with our dog. I took him in the car one morning and sat on a bench at a well-known lookout spot. It was whale migration season, and I sat in awe as I watched the whales, so large yet graceful. This was the 'serenity' I'd heard others talk about.

To protect my two husbands (I'll introduce my second husband later), I will not give details of the ups and downs or the good, the bad, and the ugly. This is not a game of blame and shame. Suffice it to say, my first marriage ended when I was about eighteen months sober. I barely slept or ate, so I went to see my GP, who put me on antidepressants and a small dosage of Valium to help me sleep.

I realise how hard it must have been living with me in active addiction, and I remember my husband saying how he would turn the key in the front door in fear of what he would find. I would be either in a manic state, singing in the midst of meal preparation, or passed out on the couch totally drunk.

I arrived at an AA meeting one night, distraught, and sat on a bench outside with a lovely old man who was the official welcoming party. He was always there, despite relapsing every few months. He smoked, so I asked him for a cigarette. He refused, saying, 'Why start now? You haven't smoked for nearly twenty years.' I sobbed and begged him. He finally gave in, and there began my new vice.

My weekly attendance at the local Baptist church and Bible study with a small group of women were crucial to my emotional and spiritual recovery. The sense of belonging, safety, support, and closeness to God carried me through the incredibly hard times and allowed me to fully appreciate the wonder of being alive. I loved being a part of the weekly women's group. We would meet at someone's house, supposedly to study the Bible, which did happen briefly. Our time together, though, was more like group therapy. We would talk and pray about our various problems and share lots of laughs.

With all that was going on, AA was my lifeline. Meetings in Sydney were quite different from those I'd attended in the United Kingdom. A member who welcomed people at the door wrote down everyone's names and gave the list to the chairperson, who would call people out to the front to share. This was very difficult in the beginning. I was crippled with anxiety and often said very little, bursting into tears. Everyone always clapped, and I would sit down. A lovely older man explained why there were two chairs at the front. One was for the person sharing if he or she wanted to sit down, and the other was for God. I believe it's true. God is present in all the meetings. It was pointed out to me early on that AA was a *we* programme. The first word of step one is *we*. Where else could you go to be heard and understood, supported, and encouraged? For me, the only other place is church, and time spent with people who understand my struggle. I need all three.

A few weeks after Christmas came the huge day of my ex-husband leaving to work in Asia and our son leaving to travel for four months before starting University in Edinburgh. Now it was me and my beautiful daughter, who really needed me.

My ex-husband would come to Sydney nearly every month and rent an apartment so that he and our daughter could have quality time together.

My sleeping had been a problem since getting sober, and I'd lose interest in food very easily if unsettled. His visits, although lovely for him and my daughter, left me feeling lonely, heartbroken, and longing to be a family again. I decided to go to a nearby large medical centre, hoping to get some Valium. I couldn't go to my GP, as I knew she wouldn't prescribe me anymore. This is how my 'doctor shopping' for Valium began. The doctor I saw was sympathetic and, to my amazement, prescribed me a pot of fifty Valium tablets. I honestly did not intend to abuse them at that time and did just use them for my anxiety and to help me sleep.

When I was two years sober, my sponsor suggested it was time for me to sponsor people. I was excited at the idea. Within a week, I was sponsoring a younger woman who had a five-year-old and a newborn. She rang me at lunchtime one day, drunk, and asked me to come over, which I did. The baby was asleep. As we sat chatting, she kept disappearing to the bathroom. I knew she was drinking, so I asked her if she could slow it down. Her daughter was due to be picked up from a private school a few suburbs away. She asked me to drive her and the baby. I agreed. We arrived for the pickup late. I told her to stay in the car, but she insisted on getting out and fell onto the curb. Her daughter looked confused, and I told her I was a friend of her mum's and that her mum wasn't feeling well.

The same thing happened a few days later. Again I went over. She was passed out on the couch, and the baby was screaming downstairs. I managed to wake her up and encouraged her to ring her husband. She refused and wanted me to pick up her daughter. Just then, my daughter, whose school was only ten minutes away, rang me. She'd filled her car up with petrol, but there wasn't enough money in her account to pay for it. I told the woman I had to leave. She was furious and verbally abusive.

I told my sponsor what had happened. She pointed out that I'd done too much; a sponsor is someone who supports, not enables. I never again saw or heard from the woman whom I had attempted to sponsor.

My second attempt at sponsorship was a big mistake. She had gone through loads of sponsors, all of whom she had manipulated, and my sponsor recommended I decline. I decided I would sponsor her anyway. She was young and very attractive. She flirted with men in AA and was living with an older man, who was also in AA. This, I thought, was a bit strange and unprofessional; he was taking advantage of her vulnerability.

Our first meeting was in a coffee shop.

'So how's this going to work with you and me?' she asked.

I was rather taken aback but said all I would like her to do was attend as many meetings as she could, ring me every day, and start working on step one.

She smiled and said, 'I have done the steps before, so there's no need.'

I told her she needed to do step one again, as she obviously didn't believe she was powerless over alcohol and her life unmanageable.

I met her a few times. She phoned up drunk numerous times, begging for help. The only advice I gave was, first, 'Go to a meeting' and, second, 'Keep your legs shut.' Sorry to be rather crude, but she was having sex with the man she was living with, as well as going out drunk and having sex with random men. That relationship ended badly. She 'sacked' me and called me a self-righteous bitch.

I stayed close to AA. I needed the continued connection and support. I began to realise how many hours in the day I had, which was such a gift compared to my days of drinking. I started volunteering at a wonderful place called Bear Cottage. It was the only children's hospice in New South Wales. My volunteer work gave me purpose, and although I was administering to children who were so ill and letting them go was extremely sad, I loved my time there. The building was at the bottom of a large grand old estate, which resembled a small version of the one on *Downton Abbey*, one of my favourite TV series.

A scene in *The Great Gatsby* was being filmed at the location, and it had been beautifully transformed. A member of the filming crew visited Bear Cottage and asked if we would like to bring some of the children up on the day the wonderful old cars were arriving. There was tremendous excitement, and a few of us took some of the older children up. I was with a teenager who was delightful and a great deal of fun to be around, despite the fact he was suffering from an incurable disease and didn't have long to live. Dragging his wheelchair through the gravel that had been laid out was difficult, but seeing the look on his face more than made up for it. We were allowed to look at all the old cars but not touch them, which my chap found nearly impossible, as they were so exquisite.

I'd spotted a new man in AA. He'd been in and out of the rooms for years and was now back in early recovery. Many AA members warned me of the dangers of dating someone who was in such early recovery, but love certainly is blind! If I'm honest, I fell in lust, not love. He was a carpenter and loved the simple things in life.

In the first few weeks of this new and exciting entanglement, life was amazing. My daughter liked him when she met him and even rated him a ten, as he looked quite like the actor Kevin Bacon. We would sit separately in AA meetings to show the other members we weren't too involved.

It wasn't long before he started staying over at my place, and this made my daughter feel uncomfortable, naturally. He then moved in, which caused even more tension with my daughter. I look back and realise how hard it must have been for her to have gone through her parents separating, her brother moving away to study at Edinburgh University, and now a man she barely knew living in our house. No longer could she feel free and able to wander around in her undies and singlet top. Before his arrival in our lives, my daughter and I loved our nights in, watching films and eating pasta and loads of chocolate.

The marriage would last just over three months, after which my daughter and I would have our special time back, which was priceless. She was so easy to live with and encouraged me to get to meetings. Her friends would come and hang out to keep her company, and nine times out of ten, they baked yummy biscuits or cakes.

My second husband and I got married very soon after meeting. In hindsight, I see that I wanted desperately to be loved and have a new soul mate. Rather than go into the gory details, I'll simply say that after two months he began drinking and taking drugs. I suffered extreme abuse from him, and I ended the marriage.

My ex-husband who was living in Malaysia made sure he was involved in our kids' lives. He flew our son in from Edinburgh and our daughter up from Sydney for a ten-day stay. He excelled as a dad, for which I was so grateful. I know for a fact that we have always been united for our kids, and neither of us ever entered into bad-mouthing each other. That, in my book, is *priceless*.

I was still attending four or five AA meetings a week. I needed them, as my recovery had been one drama after another. I often heard people share about alcoholics having big egos. I didn't think this applied to me. It struck me during a meeting that I did have a big ego. I would sit in meetings planning to give the 'perfect' share.

At one meeting, I stood up and shared in my usual 'Miss AA' way, getting loads of laughs, and then sat down feeling pleased with my share. The next person who shared was an older man who had been sober a long time. I found him quite boring, as I knew his story word for word. But he ended by saying, 'To all the newcomers, I urge you to take the cotton wool out of your ears and place it in your mouth.'

Oh shit. I was convinced his words were meant for me. I felt paranoid and refused to share for almost a month. It was true I did feel rather like Miss AA, always sharing and getting lots of laughs. That was fine, but this disease was no laughing matter.

In AA, I met a lovely older woman who was a trained counsellor. She visited me one day at home. I was tormented. I told her how much shame, anger, and sadness I felt about my two failed marriages and how I worried terribly what people would think. I loved her reply. 'What other people think of you is none of your business.'

It was a huge revelation. I'd spent my whole life seeking approval from others and trying to look and act 'perfect'. How *exhausting*! She also said 'no' is a complete sentence and that anything after 'but' is very often bullshit. This rang true for me. I had found saying no to be one of the most difficult things, so I always added 'but', followed by an elaborate, often fabricated explanation.

Towards the end of the year, I decided to enrol in a twelve-month course. At the end of the course, I would receive a Certificate IV in Alcohol, Drugs, and Mental Health. I was sure I would end up working in a rehab centre. I hadn't studied or worked in years, and the course involved assignments that were to involve preparing them on my computer and printing them out. This terrified me, as I was and still am pretty useless on the computer.

The first half of the course went surprisingly well. I loved it and got top marks on all my work. It was around March that our gorgeous golden retriever went missing overnight. His disappearance was utterly baffling. He never left my side and would sit next to me as I gardened and never ran away. My daughter was naturally devastated and printed out posters with his picture and our contact details. We spent hours covering a huge area, sticking her signs to street lamp posts and anything that would be visible.

Every morning, I would go out searching for him. AA members also joined the search, but we never found him. On the fourth day, I received a phone call from a vet in a nearby suburb. He had been found and was ready to be picked up. I was so thrilled. When I arrived, I could hear him sounding distressed. Finally, he was brought out to me. It was bliss, despite the fact he was covered in blood and mud. He was so pleased to see me, and I drove him home.

My daughter was asleep, so I decided I would wash him and then wake her up. He loved his washes. I shampooed him, rubbed his tummy over and over again, and then began to hose him down. He collapsed on me, and huge volumes of blood started pouring out of his mouth. He died in my arms. Two veterinary nurses came to take him away. Watching them zip up the body bag was devastating. The last thing I saw was his face.

I had to wake my daughter. She was initially angry that I hadn't woken her as soon as he was home. I explained I hadn't wanted her to see him in that state, and she calmed down. I rang my ex-husband, who was devastated. This dog had been part of the family, and for me, he had been my 'recovery partner'. His death left me broken-hearted and led to another trip to the medical centre to get a pot of fifty Valium. When I rang our son to share the news, he was sad but philosophical. 'At least he made it home and died in your arms,' he said. Such wisdom for someone so young.

Part of the divorce settlement included our daughter and me living in the family home for three years, and the period was due to end in September. We decided to put the home on the market sooner, as we were advised that it was a good time to sell. My AA meetings dropped off. I was going to about two or three a week. My coursework needed doing, and then there was the selling of the house and looking for somewhere for my daughter to live.

Dad's health was failing, and he was taken into hospital early June. He had an ulcerated foot and the infection was spreading up his leg. The doctors decided to do a skin graft from his thigh to his lower leg. I knew he would never survive this. But it seemed his doctors thought they had to try something. I booked a date to fly back with my daughter. We were to arrive on 27 June. I was in almost daily contact with my sister or Mum, and it seemed as though he was responding well to the antibiotics.

I'll never forget the day Mum rang me and told me Dad had died. My daughter was staying with her dad in an apartment in Sydney, and our son was studying in Edinburgh. We sobbed down the phone, and I said I would bring our flights forward. But Mum rightly said, 'No. Stick to your original flight.' She knew that flying filled with such grief could well cause me to pick up a drink.

I rang my ex-husband, who was wonderful. He was always good in a crisis and knew me so well. He said exactly what I needed to hear and how we should tell the kids. I went over to have dinner with him and our daughter the following night, and he had arranged a Skype call with our son. I knew how much our kids adored their granddad, or 'Bump' as they called him. This was going to be devastating.

We told our daughter of my Dad's death first and then our son over Skype. Their reactions were strikingly different. Our daughter sobbed, and our son just sat staring at us in total disbelief.

I left and went straight to an AA meeting, where the support was great. But nothing could console me.

My ex-husband would have loved to be at the funeral but had to stay in Sydney, as the house was on the market. It needed to look good for the open house inspections, which were twice a week.

My daughter and I flew to the UK and caught the train down to Wales. My son arrived later that day. I can still remember how I felt walking into the house. No Dad and feelings of grief so huge it was unbearable. I wandered around the house looking at pictures and sat in Dad's office, which was extremely quirky, rather like Aladdin's cave.

Mum was amazingly strong as she told me about the phone call from the hospital at around 6 a.m. the morning Dad died. The hospital told her that she should come quickly, so she picked up my sister and drove over. Dad had been dead for a short while, and we thanked God that he had died peacefully in his sleep. I felt so sad that I hadn't managed to give him a final hug. But as we chatted, I realised that Dad died knowing he was so loved by us all, and this gave me some comfort.

Dad's funeral was arranged quickly. It was a true celebration of his life, and all the many people who came to pay their respects reflected on what an amazing man Dad was. Dad, in his adorable childlike way, had always loved the cartoon character Tigger and had three stuffed Tiggers.

It was decided that one would sit among the beautiful lilies on his coffin. This caused a lot of amusement. My nephew gave an amazing eulogy about his grandfather, who had been a mentor to him. My brother also gave a wonderful eulogy. It was from the heart and funny, and he also sang a pitch-perfect song, 'Guide me, O thou great Redeemer'.

I sobbed throughout the beautiful hymns, but deep down knew God had 'rescued' Dad at just the right time, he was now with our heavenly father, whole and free of pain and suffering.

There is a wonderful Christian retreat centre, which overlooks a stunning beach not far from where Mum and Dad lived. Mum and Dad had been very involved there. Dad was a trustee, and both he and Mum had been involved in prayer ministry. The centre graciously provided an amazing buffet after the funeral and cremation. People spilled out into the beautiful gardens and talked with such love and respect about Dad.

When we finally got home, we were exhausted and had an early night. At this point, I was taking large amounts of Valium to get through it all, and it never crossed my mind that I had 'switched the witch for the bitch', which is an AA saying. I realised years later that I hadn't allowed myself to feel the full extent of the devastating events which had occurred while drinking or sober—the death of my gorgeous Dad, the breakdown of my two marriages, the deaths of our beautiful dogs, the extreme worry and pain I'd caused my loved ones, and the extent of my self-hatred, which had led to my attempt suicide. I'd anaesthetised myself with alcohol, Valium, and other drugs later on.

I had already planned for my sister to come and stay in Sydney in August. I watched Mum get overwhelmed by all the visitors who kept popping in, so I asked her if she would like to fly out with my sister. She agreed straight away, and within hours, the flights were booked. I flew back with my daughter. Our house looked like a show house, with furniture staged and everything immaculate.

The house sold quickly, which was great, but this meant I had to find somewhere for me and my daughter to live. I was still studying, so my time for viewing properties was limited. I had decided that I would indulge us and find somewhere nice, which I did. It was a lovely apartment overlooking Manly Beach and perfect for the two of us.

My Mum and sister came to visit as planned. We were still in the family home. Their stay was mixed. Mum was exhausted, and we were all grieving Dad. Mum and my sister would take themselves off sightseeing when I was in college. I know this was painful for Mum, as she was revisiting places that she and Dad had visited. My Valium intake had increased. I had managed to get more and was taking a lot during their stay.

My daughter's eighteenth birthday fell during their stay. My son flew in unexpectedly, which was lovely. My daughter announced she would like a big family dinner on the night of her birthday. This filled me with fear and dread, as I knew it would mean meeting my ex-husband's partner for the first time.

My daughter's birthday arrived. I spent hours cooking and making the house look beautiful. I was so grateful to have my Mum and sister there for support. Mum sat chatting with my former in-laws, and my sister was her usual bubbly and friendly self.

Even though I say it myself, the evening went really well, and meeting the new partner was easier than expected. Mum and my sister left, which was hard. But I knew I would see them at Christmas, as I'd already booked flights back. We moved into the apartment with great excitement. I gave my daughter the main bedroom with an en-suite, as I wanted her to have space for friends coming for sleepovers and the like. My bedroom was small but fine, and I had a bathroom next to it. The views from the small balcony were stunning, and I would have my first mug of tea and cigarette out there, thinking how amazing life was. My daughter had her own little car, which had been her brother's, so she was always dashing off here, there, and everywhere or having friends over. I completed my studies, and for the first time in ages, I felt proud of myself and hopeful for the future.

My daughter struggled with her final exams, which wasn't surprising given all she had been through. At the end of every school year, her school had a 'prize-giving' evening. Students were awarded books for coming first in various subjects and went onto the stage to receive them. The recipients were always the same students. Afterwards, my daughter would say to me, 'Are you disappointed I wasn't on stage?'

My answer was always honest. I would tell her how proud I was of her sporting achievements and how I loved reading her school reports, which always said she was a delight to teach and caring towards others but could try harder academically. She was so similar to me at her age—I had played hockey and netball for my school but could have done better in exams if I'd studied properly.

My daughter announced she would like to study in the United Kingdom like her brother had, which was fine. But I realised that meant I would need to move back myself. I couldn't bear the thought of being 12,000 miles away from both my kids and thought, *It's now or never*. So I planned my move for the middle of the following year.

I doctor shopped once more as our first Christmas without Dad approached. Mum was amazing and did everything exactly the same as it always had been. Dad loved Christmas, especially the large collection of singing, dancing soft toys that sat on the piano. I have to say I had given him most of them and sat sobbing as I put the batteries back in them that year.

We chose a day to scatter Dad's ashes. My brother had looked at the weather forecast and checked the direction of the wind. After lunch, we went in convoy to a beautiful beach. Mum and Dad had a lease on one of the beach huts, and it was a special place with so many happy memories. We chose a spot on the side of a cliff. My brother gave us all a plastic cup with some of Dad's ashes in it. It's all a bit unreal when I look back. A beautiful prayer was said for Dad, and we separated and went in different directions. My kids were so supportive. We wandered down a small cliff and sat there clutching our cups. I said a prayer, and then we gently scattered darling Dad over grass and rocks.

It was a sad farewell as my daughter and I set off for the flight back to Sydney. The Valium had helped me through, and I honestly believe I would have passed a lie detector test if asked if I had any intention of drinking alcohol on the flight back.

I had so much knowledge about this disease. I had read the AA Big Book three times. I'd been through the steps twice, had sponsored two women, and had just completed a course in alcohol and drugs. Knowledge will not keep you sober, as I was about to find out.

The first leg of the journey was fine. We stopped in Dubai for a few hours and then started on the second leg of the journey. My daughter fell asleep. I watched a sad film and was crying when a stewardess came up and asked me if I was all right.

Without any thought, the words that came out were, 'I'll have a double vodka tonic please.'

Without realising it, I had absolutely no mental defence against my disease when those words came out of my mouth. I don't remember the film I watched, but I drank excessively until a few hours before we were due to land.

I was disgusted with myself and desperately trying to sober up. I remember thinking, *That didn't count. I was in the air. And I'll put a stop to this straight away.*

This of course didn't happen. I had put alcohol into my body, which triggered the physical craving. It was worse than when I had finally got sober, nearly four years earlier.

CHAPTER 4

DEFIANT TO THE END

This disease is indeed progressive. Even though I had been sober all that time, it wasn't long before the consequences got far worse than ever before (apart from the suicide attempt, which should have been enough to make me stop). I was now drinking until I would black out. It wasn't all the time at first, but it ended up that way fourteen months later.

I went to my home group AA meeting during that first week and proudly shared how I had resisted alcohol during the flight. I felt very relieved. I had a bottle of wine in my car ready to get stuck into after the meeting.

This continued for a few weeks. I carefully planned my post–AA meeting drinking. I would have two glasses in a plastic cup before I drove home. I knew there was a spot on my route that was notorious for pulling over random cars for RBT (random breath testing). Once past that spot, I would stop on a side street, polish off the rest, and continue drinking at home.

It was wine. I was not drinking vodka this time. Maybe in my sick mind, I thought it was safer and only a few grapes! I hid the bottles in my wardrobe behind clothes. But one awful morning, I was knocking back a glass of wine in my bathroom when my daughter walked in. I shall never forget the look on her face and the crippling guilt, shame, and remorse I felt.

I nonetheless continued to drink, and one day I decided to move a heavy wooden box down to our storeroom. I was in a sundress and flip-flops as I went down hard concrete stairs. I must have caught my flip-flops on the stairs and fell, landing on the hard box. I had no idea what damage I'd done so carried on and put the box in the storeroom.

It was then that I looked down and saw I was covered in blood. I went straight to the bathroom and, to my horror, saw that my upper lip was split all the way through. I managed to drive to the local hospital, pressing a tea towel on my lip.

I arrived around 7 p.m. The doctor took one look at it and said I needed plastic surgery the next day. My daughter was due to be dropped off by her dad that night. I had texted them from the hospital to tell them what had happened, leaving out the fact I'd been drinking.

The following day, I drove drunk to meet the plastic surgeon, who booked me in that afternoon. I needed three layers of stitches, and the surgeon said I'd been extremely lucky, as the split was virtually dead centre and even now is barely visible.

I was busted. My ex-husband knew I'd been drunk when the accident occurred, so I agreed to book back into the rehab I had been to four years earlier. This was serious. My detox was horrific, and the all-consuming guilt and shame were unbearable. I had to go to AA meetings where the attendees knew me and stand up and ID myself, sharing however many days sober I was. They all clapped and were very supportive. I was asked to 'share' at every meeting. I guess it was to show how powerful this disease is. But after a while, I was too exhausted to share, so I declined.

I was under the care of the same psychiatrist I had been nearly four years previously. She looked pleasantly surprised to see me, admitting I was one of her cases whose death wouldn't have surprised her if she'd heard about it. My intense denial and the seemingly blasé way I brushed aside my suicide attempt and other deluded beliefs had led her to think this. We met weekly for an hour, and as I poured out all that happened prior to my relapse, she suggested I had a lot of unresolved grief and resentments, which she wanted me to start working through straight away. The first thing she asked me to do was write a farewell letter to my Dad. It took me nearly two weeks, sobbing, writing, scrabbling it up, and throwing it in the bin numerous times. She sat and listened as I read it out during our third session. Writing it had been hard enough, but while reading it out, my heart rate was so high. I felt convinced the pain was going to lead to either a heart attack or cause a total mental breakdown. She explained the six stages of grief: denial, isolation, anger, bargaining, depression, and acceptance. This made total sense to me as I looked back over my recovery, during which I'd experienced the first five, but I had not reached the acceptance part. She also explained these phases can rotate, requiring them to be revisited many times before achieving acceptance. Despite her incredible help, as my disease progressed, I would experience the first five in the extreme, which I believe became one of the biggest reasons it took me so long to finally be honest, reach out for help, and work through my unresolved grief as well as resentments. She put it to me that I had incredible insight into my disease and a noticeable skill for descriptive and powerful writing. So much so, she suggested I could write a book and gave me details of a publishing company in America. I was flattered, and I thanked her, but the idea was way beyond my comprehension.

My daughter was due to go travelling in March, and she was so excited. For her sake, I remained sober. But I knew in my heart I would drink when she left. I had already phoned the rehab and asked to be put on the waiting list.

Saying goodbye to our daughter was hard and made even worse by the fact that my ex-husband arrived at the airport with his partner. I don't blame him. He had every right to be there, as I was already a ticking time bomb. We sat and ate dinner together, and then the time came to say our goodbyes. All I could think was how much I wanted this to be over so I could leave and get a drink.

It was a Sunday night, and I knew there was only one bottle shop open until 10 p.m. near where I lived, so I raced home and made it just in time. I started drinking straight from the first bottle of wine in the car. I had bought three bottles.

I only managed one bottle that night. I was exhausted and angry and fell asleep on the couch. I woke up early the next morning and started on the second bottle. I sat in my daughter's room and cried inconsolably. The 'mummy guilt' was all back, and I started imagining what awful things might happen to her while travelling.

I was on the third bottle and decided to have a cigarette on the balcony. I had often watched people power walking or jogging and happy women pushing prams. I didn't get to see any of that, as I tripped on the way out onto the balcony, fell against the table, and heard smashing glass. The table was on its side, the glass candle holder had smashed, and I was on my hands and knees, hearing people shout, 'Are you OK?'

'Yes,' I replied.

I was sweeping the glass when the phone rang. It was someone from the rehab centre saying they had a bed for me. Could I be there by 11? I said yes, but it was already nine. I packed the best I could, finished off the wine, and then got a taxi to the centre.

I told everyone I was in for relapse prevention, which, at the time, I thought they believed. I decided to extend my stay by two days, as I was about to turn fifty and knew waking up alone that day at home would definitely lead me to drink.

I have to be honest and say that, towards the end of my stay, I knew I was going to drink. I met a man the same age as me during my last week. We got on well, and there was definite chemistry between us. We exchanged numbers before I left.

My birthday was fun. I was allowed out with my best girlfriend. We had lunch, and I had received flowers from numerous people. In the evening we were allowed to have a 'disco' in the garden. Most of the other clients were young and had no idea what a disco was but kindly joined in, and I and a few men my age showed them how to dance 80s style. It was such fun, and we all agreed it was amazing to feel like this without any mood-altering drugs in our system. I knew, however, that I would drink the following day, and I did.

The next few months were a living hell. I was drinking more than ever and lying to everyone. I can remember lying on the couch with the air conditioner on full, thinking, *If I were a dog, I'd put myself down to end the pain and suffering.*

I had some moments of what I thought were 'clarity', one of which was to change a light bulb. Great idea, unless you were drunk, and I was. I slipped and caught just under my chin on the stepladder. There was quite a lot of blood. I dressed the wound and returned to the same local hospital. The staff already knew me, and when my details got put in the system, some kind of red flag was raised. The doctor who saw me said very little and stitched it in a rush without giving me a local anaesthetic, which has left me with a crooked scar.

I had been drinking as usual one morning and remembered the man I'd met in rehab. I texted him, and we arranged for me to go to his place for dinner that night. He was still sober and excited about seeing me. He had no idea I was drinking. I stopped to buy a bottle of vodka before arriving at his place. He looked shocked to see me obviously drunk and, worse, holding a bottle of vodka.

We drank the vodka. I had caused him to relapse, which is such a shameful thing. The night is slightly blurry, but I knew what had happened and felt awful remorse for this poor man. We both continued to drink and stay in contact. He desperately wanted us to meet up again, but I told him I couldn't see him again because I was trying to get sober—the ultimate act of selfishness, and a total lie.

I barely saw my lovely friends. I would cancel on them last minute with some fabricated story, often that I was meeting up with my sponsor or doing extra AA meetings. There were no more dinners or lunches. It had to be early-morning coffees so I could start drinking as soon as possible. I would have promised myself the previous night I would have enough wine for the morning but would wake up having drunk it all. I would then drive to the nearest bottle shop, buy my wine, and drink at least half a bottle from a plastic cup before I got home.

My sponsor and quite a few women in AA were trying to convince me to postpone my move back. They knew I was drinking but said nothing, but I was determined to stick to my plan and deluded myself into thinking I would be able to cut right back once I arrived in Wales.

In my crazy drinking, I managed to arrange an international moving company to ship my stuff back to Wales. I had booked a serviced apartment to stay in during my last week. I barely remember the packers coming in. I was in the apartment drunk.

I woke up one afternoon reaching for a drink when I saw blood all over the wall. When I looked in the mirror, I saw that my hair was matted with blood. I had a shocking headache, so I called an ambulance and went to a larger hospital. My head was scanned, and the doctors found two large haemorrhages on my brain. I couldn't even tell them how it had happened.

The consultant knew by then I was an alcoholic and told me to postpone my flight by a week, adding that on no account should I drink, especially on the plane. The cabin pressure could kill me. I would love to now say that was my 'rock bottom'. But sadly, no. I had many more to come.

I continued drinking, avoiding girlfriends and AA, and I can't remember much about the last week before I flew. I did manage to change my flight and kept praying I would stop drinking. This was *serious*.

When I checked in at the airport, someone with the airline explained the flight had been overbooked in business class so I had been upgraded to first class on the second leg of the journey, which was the longest part. I was thrilled and dashed to the lounge to drink endless glasses of Champagne before boarding the plane. I had more Champagne before we took off and then countless more glasses before we landed in Malaysia, where I was due to change planes. I went straight to the first class lounge, which was incredible. I have no idea how many drinks I consumed, but know I nearly missed the flight. The attendants were calling me by name. I settled into my first-class seat and was immediately offered Champagne. I continued drinking, knowing I could die on the plane.

When I landed at Heathrow, my head felt as if it was going to explode. But that didn't stop me buying a few bottles of wine for the drive down to Wales in a hire car. Three hours of motorway driving later—God was most certainly protecting me and all the other drivers—and I made it to a one-bedroom holiday let that I had rented in advance for two months. I somehow managed to drag my cases in. I felt sick—my headache was excruciating and I was finding it difficult to see or stand up.

I knew I was in trouble and called an ambulance and then phoned my sister and said I was off to hospital. She met me there soon after I'd arrived, and her support and love were what carried me through the four days of detoxing and crippling fear as I waited for my brain scan results.

The consultant approached my bed not looking very happy. *This is it,* I thought.

But another miraculous intervention from our loving God—the haemorrhages were the same size as they had been in Sydney. Surely it was time to put an end to my drinking once and for all? I had been detoxed, experienced a miracle, and felt physically the best I'd felt in months. Great—time to see if I could just have a few drinks and enjoy the excitement of moving back! Within two days I was drinking as much as before the hospitalisation.

The plan was to buy a house and move in once my things arrived from Sydney. I was still drinking 24/7 on the days I could get away with it and decided to house hunt. I made sure the viewings were mid-morning so I was at least fairly 'with it'. I only saw two houses and bought the first one I saw. This was my biggest drunken purchase ever, but I believe without any doubt that God went before me, as my house is lovely, just the right size, and in a great location. Plus, I have wonderful neighbours both sides who know my 'battle'.

My mum knew a woman who worked at a local drug and alcohol centre and suggested I go along for help. I managed to slow my drinking down enough to enrol in an eleven-week addiction awareness course. The class met once a week and only lasted a few hours. I sat bored throughout the lectures. After all, I wasn't just the 'Rehab Queen'; I already knew all the stuff being presented to us. I'd studied it during my course in Sydney while sober.

I then moved into a small 'process group'. There were about six of us. We met up weekly and talked about our addictions. Again, I found this boring and painful to sit through, knowing I had wine in my car ready to drink when I left.

The centre also ran activities Monday through Friday. I looked at the sheet and, in a state of deluded grandeur, thought, *What sort of people need to fill their days with these things? Don't they have lives?* Of course, my life was *perfect*—*not*. I was a chronic alcoholic.

I moved into my new house. I drank as usual with no sense of shame. I didn't care what the men who were putting all the furniture in the right rooms thought. In fact, I never did care when I drank. I had lost any sense of pride and would return to the same shops day after day to buy my booze. When the movers had finished, I was utterly relieved to see them go so I could drink to oblivion. After all, it was my first night in my new home.

Mum and my sister came over for quite a few evening meals. On those days, I would drink two bottles of wine first thing in the morning, sleep, and then be ready for them (eye drops in and perfume sprayed). I would sweat and blame it on the menopause, a total lie. I had been through that two years previously. I don't know why I was surprised to learn that they and everyone else knew I was drinking.

My brother, his wife, and their three daughters were staying with my Mum, and I invited them for dinner. The evening was going well. Everyone enjoyed the meal, and then their youngest daughter suggested a game of hide-and-seek. I sat terrified, desperately trying to remember where I'd hidden wine bottles.

I thought I'd got away with it and got stuck into the wine after they'd gone. I hadn't got away with it. My brother's, wife who is very petite, had hidden in one of the wardrobes and found a bottle. I didn't find this out until a few weeks later.

Distraught by the fact my lies weren't working anymore, I drank to blackout for three days. Nothing seemed to be working anymore. I was covered in unexplained bruises and felt as though I was having a heart attack, so I called an ambulance. Two paramedics arrived, one of whom I remembered from school.

I was taken by ambulance to hospital. The wait was four hours to be seen by a doctor. It was hell, and all I wanted was to be detoxed. By the time the doctor saw me, I was beginning to sober up and desperate for a drink. So I walked out, got a taxi home, stopping at a petrol station for more wine, and passed out on the couch after the first bottle.

A few days after the aborted hospital visit, my daughter, who had been studying in Brighton, texted me and said she had made a terrible mistake and that she wanted to move back to Australia. I was crushed and heartbroken but said it was fine, as all I wanted was for her to be happy.

I saw her off on the train at 5 p.m. on a Sunday and then went straight to my sister's for what I thought was going to be a commiseration dinner with Mum there. It wasn't. I arrived sobbing and dying for a drink. My sister spoke her truth about how my drinking was killing Mum and her and told me how she lived in constant fear that I would kill someone while drink driving. She said I loved booze more than God, my family, and even my own kids. She was right. Alcoholism had hardened my heart and robbed me of any feelings. Once alcohol was inside me, nothing and nobody else mattered. It was my 'God'.

My sister then came to sit next to me on the couch and said, 'Here is the sister who loves and cares about you.' I sobbed, and she hugged me tightly.

Mum was firm and fair but reiterated the fact that only I could beat this affliction. She was right, but the mental obsession was so great I had no chance of beating it. I was hopelessly gridlocked.

I left and drank to oblivion. The second hospitalisation was far more dramatic. I decided in the morning to drive down to the beach where we'd scattered Dad's ashes and drink while I chatted to him. I have no recollection of what happened. I woke up in hospital, and the horrendous truth unravelled. I had been found slumped over the steering wheel of my car. A woman had called the police and ambulance. The police couldn't charge me, as the keys weren't in the ignition. My poor Mum had two policemen at her door telling her what had happened. I can't imagine the fear and desperation she must have felt at the realisation of how sick I was.

While detoxing in hospital, I thought, *This really is the final straw.* Mum and my sister knew a woman who worked in a long-term Christian rehab. My sister came in with the forms, which I signed. Quite honestly, I was desperate and ashamed and would have signed anything to keep them happy. My sister went out of her way to protect and help me. She moved in with me until a spot opened up for me.

It was a ten-month programme, and at the time, I really believed I needed to be removed from life in order to get sober. My Mum dropped me off at the facility. I was hopeful but chronically depressed at the thought of not being able to speak to anyone in the first month or have visitors for three months.

The first week was OK. I was excused from any duties or study and allowed to watch films. I liked the principle of this place. None of us called ourselves addicts, and we were going to be 'set free' by God during our stay. The daily routine was rigid, with allocated jobs and expected standards, which, if not met, resulted in a warning, which came in the form of a white ticket and meant extra kitchen duties.

Most of the girls were very young and had lived horrific lives on the streets, eating out of bins, being abused, and selling their bodies to survive and feed their addictions. As a result, they hadn't learnt any life skills. I could see how our daily tasks could benefit them but not *me*. I had lived a life. I had been a nurse, a wife, and a mother, and I knew how to run a home and the importance of basic skills like showering daily and brushing your teeth. I need to add that in no way did I feel superior to the other clients.

I was sharing a room with a young woman who seemed to take an instant dislike to me. She had experienced a terrible life and accused me one morning of not being a 'real alcoholic', adding that I didn't deserve a bed at the facility. She called me a 'stuck-up bitch.' I reported this to the staff, and it wasn't resolved.

I became increasingly angry, especially with the 'white ticket' business. A staff member would knock and then enter our rooms at 7 a.m. If our feet weren't actually on the ground, we got a white ticket. We had to empty our bin first thing in the morning. Our rooms were checked around 8 a.m. One morning, my roommate and I got a white ticket for a facial wipe in our bin! She had put it there just before morning prayer and meditation. *How ludicrous*, I thought.

The ten months were looming before me, and I was feeling desperately 'trapped' and crippled with anxiety. I just wanted to get out and live my life. I decided I would leave after ten days but had to ring my Mum as next of kin. She told me I hadn't given it a chance and that I should stay, so I did.

It was coming up to Christmas, and the house was full of excitement as we decorated trees and hung decorations. But I was miserable and angry and made my mind up to 'definitely' leave. I'd confided in one of my peers, who must have informed the staff.

I kept trying to see the manager, but she wouldn't see me. So I slipped a note under her door, telling her I was leaving. The staff kept me busy. It was all a ploy to stall me leaving, as it was difficult to discharge people after 5 p.m.

Finally, I banged on the manager's door, marched in, and told her I was leaving. She said she had no idea I had been trying to talk to her, which was an outright lie. I could see my note in front of her. I again had to ring my Mum, who was once again understandably angry. I told her nobody could stop me leaving and hung up.

The staff dragged my discharge out. My anger turned to rage, and I finally managed to leave in disgrace. I was escorted to the taxi under my coat so the other clients wouldn't witness this shameful act.

I was determined to prove everyone wrong, and didn't drink the first night. I was relieved I could smoke again and drank loads of tea and ginger beer.

The following morning, I had no intention of drinking. I booked a massage and a trip to the beautician. I was going to text my son later to wish him luck in his exams. This never happened. I went to the local shops and bought two large bottles of vodka. I drank to blackout for four days. My Mum and sister dropped in a few times to see if I was OK. I can only imagine the fear they endured each time they visited. I realised not long after that they had fully expected to find me dead.

They visited during my last day of blackout drinking, and to this day I have no recollection of the visit or my incredibly destructive words and behaviour. I was in bed with a half-drunk huge bottle of vodka by my bedside. I woke up at 5 a.m., checked my phone, and saw numerous text messages from my sister. The messages said I had abused her verbally, said terrible things, and told her to 'Fuck off' repeatedly. Apparently Mum was sobbing next to my bed, and I was begging her to help me. She had left a note on the kitchen top with a picture of Dad and me during their last and final visit to Sydney. She had also put a small wooden cross next to it. I have never felt so ashamed. I sobbed, cradling the picture of Dad and me and thinking how incredibly sad he would be looking down at me.

I had alcoholic poisoning. I threw up violently from 5 a.m. and could barely stand up. I managed to shower, still vomiting, and then sank into the couch, thinking, *This really is my rock bottom*—which, yet again, was sadly not the case.

Another ambulance ride, followed by a long wait in casualty preceded my third admission, so I decided to fake a seizure to get the doctors' attention. I was admitted to a ward, and detox began.

The staff were lovely and in no way judgemental. I guess I was low maintenance, as I could shower myself and even changed my own sheets while detoxing. I was visited by a lovely man I had met during my previous admission. He was high up in the drug and alcohol field and had warned me of the dangers of my chronic alcoholism.

My son arrived and was staying with my Mum. I hated myself so much that I didn't want to see anyone. But Mum visited one day, which was nice. I told her that the drug and alcohol man was coming back the following day, and she requested to be present.

She arrived with my son, who was wonderful. We went for a coffee and cigarette, and he kept hugging me and telling me how much he loved me. I could see the pain and fear in his eyes, which crushed my heart. The man arrived with the doctor and discussed the seriousness of my condition. My Mum was desperate and asked him what she could do. He advised her to take away my car keys and money. At this point, she looked slightly more relieved and said, 'Thank you. I've been so worried about her drink driving.'

The doctor asked me if I had driven while drunk, and I lied, saying I really didn't know. There was a new law in place, and the doctor informed me he would have to contact the DVLA. He was legally obliged to do so. I was in the process of getting my old paper licence changed with an updated photo ID and felt sure the licence would be granted, as I hadn't actually been caught drink driving. This wasn't the case. My licence was suspended and would only be issued once I'd been sober for twelve months.

The doctor and the drug and alcohol expert left. *Mamma Mia!* was on the TV, which was torture. It had been one of my daughter's favourite films, and we had watched it loads of times and danced around. This was during my first sobriety. The Salvation Army came in and played carols for over an hour. I sat and sobbed, realising the damage and hurt I had caused my family. On my last night, *The Sound of Music* was on the TV, which was even worse. This had been one of Dad's favourite films, and we had watched it virtually every Christmas. I lay there sobbing, missing Dad terribly, and in absolute disbelief at my behaviour towards my sister, who had gone out of her way to support and care for me.

I was discharged on Christmas Eve. Frail and desperate, I went to my GP and asked him to prescribe Antabuse. I had agreed with my Mum that I would take it. It was freezing and raining as I walked to the local chemist, praying I would be able to get the prescription filled, as it was Christmas Eve. A lovely woman greeted me, saw my pain, and ordered it in. I collected it two hours later.

Mum visited with my son later that afternoon. She was relieved I'd got the Antabuse, but it had been decided that my son should stay with her. This broke my heart.

We discussed how she would give me a weekly allowance and supervise my drug taking. She then invited me to join her and the family for lunch the following day, which was totally unexpected after the way I'd treated my sister. I agreed, but truthfully, I would have preferred to sit in an imaginary hole and drown in the shit caused by my drinking.

For me the day was awful. I felt so unworthy of even being there, given the destruction and fear I had put my loved ones through. I had trouble eating, and I broke down when my son gave me a beautiful book he and his sister had been working on. On the cover was a gorgeous picture of me, tanned and healthy, taken when I was sober in Sydney. The book was full of pictures, starting with photos of me as a child that Mum had given them. It was amazing. I sat, fighting back the tears, feeling utterly unworthy but full of gratitude for my amazing kids.

Mum picked me up mid-morning on Boxing Day, and we went to hers. The following day, my brother and his family were present. Another excruciating day, feeling nothing other than crippling guilt, shame, and remorse. My son was moving in with me that day, as the beds were now full at Mum's. We were invited back the next day, and without thinking, we agreed. It wasn't until we got home that I burst into tears and told my son I couldn't do another day of it. He agreed and phoned my Mum and told her we wouldn't be coming, which was a huge relief.

It was an absolute blessing having him around. He was happy with life, loving Edinburgh, and had just finished his first year of a geology degree. This course of study was perfect for him. As a child, he had loved nature, all animals, and swimming. Whenever he went snorkelling, he loved seeing new amazing fish. Even as a toddler, and still very sick, his favourite outing was to the zoo. I would park his pushchair, and he'd spend hours watching the meerkats and chimpanzees. The house we were living in when our daughter was born had a couple of blue-tongued lizards that had decided our garden was their home. They terrified me, but our son became best friends with them and spent hours sitting on the wooden steps feeding them ham and chatting away to them.

Getting back to my 'drinking career', after my son left, one of my best friends was down, which was the only thing that kept me sane. She was so supportive and naturally very concerned, but we managed to relive our youth and have some laughs.

CHAPTER 5

HOW ON EARTH CAN I MAKE A COMEBACK FROM THAT?

Despite having had my driving licence suspended, I managed by walking everywhere or taking the buses. The supervision of my taking the Antabuse was relatively easy over the Christmas and New Year period. My son and girlfriend were able to relieve Mum most days. I knew the idea of her having to do it would prove difficult. I'd put her through so much, and she was exhausted as a result, so I arranged to have the Antabuse supervised at the local chemist. The wind, rain, and freezing conditions, and the fact it was dark by 4 p.m. made these trips a daily challenge, and I was relieved when my GP agreed I could take two tablets Monday, Wednesday, and Friday.

I decided I needed to tell my neighbours I was an alcoholic. They must have seen the ambulances outside my house. I felt like the neighbour from hell, but they were wonderful and very supportive.

I started going to the local Baptist church. The minister is a wonderful man. He ticks all the boxes for me: God's love, grace and mercy, and passion for Jesus ooze out of him, and his pastoral care is outstanding. He visited me on several occasions and still does. His prayers are always 'spot on', encouraging and insightful, providing the wonderful assurance that I am precious in God's eyes and my sins (which are off the Richter scale) have been forgiven through Jesus' death on the cross. His sense of humour blows me away. Just when I'd feel I'd never laugh again, he would come up with an appropriately hilarious comment and we would laugh together.

He has given me hope and sense of worth that can only come from God, which is priceless.

I rethought the daily activities at the drug and alcohol centre and started going. It was a huge effort to get out of bed and pluck up the courage to catch the bus there. I was crippled with anxiety. It was nothing like I'd imagined. The staff were great, and the other clients were a big support. It became a regular thing for me. Tuesdays we met at the allotment, which is behind an old castle in the village, so I could walk down and meet them there. My first trip was fun. We spent the morning filling up wheelbarrows with horse manure and putting it on the vegetable plots. I started going to personal development groups every Thursday morning, followed by auricular acupuncture.

Out of interest, I went along one Friday to check out the band they had. They asked me if I played any instruments. I told them I'd played the piano as a child. They were thrilled, as they had no one to play the keyboard. I was nervous but gave it a go, and it wasn't long before notes and chords came back to me. It felt great, and I bought myself a keyboard to practice on at home. I was only going to a few AA meetings a week. I couldn't face going out at night in the dark, so I went to lunchtime meetings. I always felt so relieved when I returned home and stepped through the front door. I felt safe and could isolate. I still like the feeling of getting home now, but it's a very different feeling. I feel safe and relax on the couch watching TV or reading.

I had a sponsor who was lovely but far too soft. I lied about having been to various AA meetings and manipulated her when it came to step work.

I am an all-or-nothing alcoholic/addict. I was either manically gardening or lying on the couch staring at the ceiling. I decided to redo the herb garden, which had been left by the previous owners. Everything was either dead or nearly dead, so I spent an entire day emptying it, including the soil. The task was backbreaking. I carried bags of soil and tipped them over the wall into the graveyard opposite my house. A few days later, I filled it with new soil—it took six large bags to fill—and then I planted way too many seedling herbs. My house, patio, driveway, and side paths had been power-washed. I spent two days painting the garden wall, barely stopping for anything to eat. I gave myself a few days off and then painted the deck and the garage door, all of which took me three days. I realise now why I did these things. I couldn't bare sitting with myself and in a crazy mind. Back when I was in my first recovery, after I told my Mum I'd walked the dog for four hours one day, she put it to me that God made us human *beings*, not human *doings*. She was right.

Despite not drinking at this point, my thinking had become totally irrational. My sister had been one of my best friends for decades. Our relationship had been full of love, trust, and laughter, and we'd supported each other through many difficult times. I order to protect her, I shall not disclose the details of what happened, something so big it hurt her beyond belief. I made a serious allegation against her, which at the time I truly believed. I even told her that God had clarified I was 'right' during my prayer time. I shudder even now, as it was the work of the 'enemy'—he was having an absolute field day with me. It wasn't until months later I was able to admit I'd been in alcoholic madness and that the allegation was totally untrue. I involved my Mum and brother, desperately wanting them to agree with me. This obsession led to me take large amounts of over-the-counter medication, such as Nytol, Sominex, codeine-based drugs, antihistamines containing a sedative, and a few others, all with the intention of numbing my mind. I knew I couldn't pick up a drink; the consequences could prove not only fatal but lead to further destruction of my relationship with loved ones.

The inevitable happened, I picked up a drink and my thinking and behaviour became indescribably worse. I began threatening my sister via text messages, demanding she own up to the allegation. I also threatened my brother, saying if he didn't side with me I would never speak to him or his family again.

As a result of my behaviour, my nephew, who I adore, let himself in the back door, which was open. I was in bed drunk but will never forget his face when he said I wasn't welcome at his wedding after what I'd put his mum through. I sobbed and begged him. The wedding had been planned for June, a week long celebration in Spain. I had already booked an apartment for me and the kids and bought a gorgeous dress, shoes, and clutch bag. This was yet another 'rock bottom', but it didn't stop me drinking.

I had all my favourite pieces of furniture, pictures, mirrors, crockery, cutlery, and the like shipped from Australia. I only needed to buy electrical items and some outdoor furniture. The outdoor furniture purchase went horribly wrong. I was drunk researching on the Internet, and all I knew was that I wanted good quality stuff, as I planned to grow old in this house. I found some beautiful rattan chocolate-coloured furniture and ordered a six-seater table with chairs and a small round table with two chairs that matched. That would have been sufficient, but in my mind, I thought I needed a larger table. I was anticipating loads of entertaining. So, proceeded to change my order, I sat with a glass of wine next to me, filling it up every ten minutes, ensuring I was drunk when I made the alteration to my order. Instead of ordering a twelve-seater table with chairs, I ordered another six-seater, plus chairs.

It all arrived. I was drunk as usual and started unwrapping it all. I was incapable of assembling the new furniture, so I left it scattered across the garden. Anybody who had seen it would have thought I had hundreds of friends and entertained a lot. The truth is, to this day, the only people who have sat on any of the outdoor furniture are myself, my son, my minister, and one of my best friends and her daughter! I'd also bought a lawn mower. I only have a small amount of grassed area and had been paying someone to come in and mow it.

I was relatively sober early one morning and looked out at the abundance of garden furniture, so I decided I would arrange to have the excess returned. The company refused to take any of it back, as I'd opened all of it. I managed to assemble the tables and put the chairs in place. But the lawnmower proved too hard, which was ridiculous—it only required screwing in eight bolts. The extra furniture is still sitting in my garage.

My drinking had reached new dangerous heights. I didn't know if it was 6 a.m. or 6 p.m. when I came to. The only way to find out the day was to look at my phone, and even then, it was hazy.

I had discovered an upmarket online shop and, again while drunk, ordered beautiful bed linen, continental pillows, pillowcases, and scatter cushions with throws to match. My bedroom looked amazing, but my bed was rarely slept in. I would wake up on the floor somewhere, or a good result would be waking up on the couch.

Towards the end of March, I got the most exciting text message in years. My daughter had given Sydney UNI a try but wanted to come back here. I was thrilled, as the only reason I'd moved back to this country was to be closer to my kids. She had gone from being vegetarian to vegan.

I woke up at 11 p.m. one night with no recollection of what had happened. I looked around the kitchen and discovered I had cooked and labelled six vegan meals, all in blackout. My food cupboards were filled excessively. I had enough cleaning products to clean probably six houses and always about thirty toilet rolls in the coat cupboard. I didn't see anything wrong with this, but during my second rehab, while discussing my kids, I realised I was still shopping as though I was in a family of four, which was absurd, as I hadn't been for quite some years. In addition to this fact, my online grocery shopping was done while drunk, so without checking my supplies I ordered anything I thought I might need.

She would be arriving just after my birthday, and the plan was for her to stay with me until university started in September. I was still drinking but knew I had to stop before she arrived so stocked up on loads of over-the-counter drugs.

When she arrived, it was wonderful. Her room was ready with welcome gifts on her bed and of course plenty of vegan food. Her stay started well. I thought she wouldn't notice anything was wrong. But of course, she did. My behaviour was erratic. I slept a lot in the day and suggested we chilled and watched 'chick flick' in order to avoid conversations of which I was surely incapable.

I couldn't understand why my daughter decided to go and stay with her brother in Edinburgh but would later realise living with me and my madness was too hard. She slept on his sitting room floor for nearly five months, never complaining, but was relieved when they moved into a flat with two friends of her brothers in September. My ex-husband's eldest sister, who lives in London, has been incredible. Both kids have gone there to stay numerous times, and she has loved them as her own. She has been their 'mum' during the many times I was totally incapable of being present for them. I am so grateful to her and her family for providing stability amidst the chaos I was living in.

I continued to drink excessively. There was no need for any drugs, as alcohol was my drug of choice. I really don't know why I wasn't more organised with my alcohol supply. After all, that's all I wanted. A good morning would be finding a half-full bottle and sipping it until I could walk up to the local shops, arriving bang on at 8 a.m., which was the time they could start selling alcohol. A seriously bad morning was realising I'd drunk it all. I would pace the house and chain smoke and often arrive at the shops around 7.30 a.m., in the hope they'd 'break the rule', which they obviously couldn't. The final straw would be waking up in the night or early hours of the morning with not a drop of alcohol in sight. I'd search my hiding spots, pulling out coats and rummaging through cupboards, all to no avail. So I would book a taxi to the 24/7 petrol station and stock up.

I was vaguely aware that things were getting progressively worse. I would wake up on the garage floor having had a cigarette or on the kitchen floor. In fact, I woke up on virtually every floor in my home. I even woke up on the patio area in the garden flat on my back. I was terrified, but pride stopped me calling out to my neighbours. I crawled on my hands and knees into the house and passed out on the sunroom floor.

You may recall how I grew up with three amazing friends. One had been living in Perth, Australia, for years and came over with her daughter for a holiday. When she visited me, I was drunk. But she said nothing other than how ill I looked. She asked me to come to Bath with our two other friends for a weekend, offering to drive. I refused, saying I needed to concentrate on my recovery—a total lie.

It was that weekend 'intervention' occurred. Everyone, my ex-husband included, knew I was in a bad way. The kids had expressed concern about me to him. Our daughter had told him that she'd texted me one morning asking if I was free to talk. I was already drunk so ignored the call, slept for three hours, and then texted her back, saying I'd been on a long coastal walk and hadn't taken my phone. What utter bullshit, and she knew it.

It was a Saturday night when the idea first took root. The girls were up late and on Facebook, and suddenly my ex-husband posted something. They hadn't been in contact with him for years but seized the opportunity to contact him. They discussed me at great lengths, feeling desperate and fearing for my life. I believe God intervened that night, and so do they. Two of them aren't Christians but felt something had led them to this. My friend returned back to Wales, visited me, and was shocked to see how frail I was and to see the bruises I'd sustained during blackout falls. My kitchen counter looked like a walk-in pharmacy. I was desperately trying to detox but failing miserably. I longed for there to be medical centres similar to the ones in Sydney so I could detox properly. The only thing that stopped me ordering Valium online was the fear of a criminal record; that would have seriously compromised my life. She convinced me to go and see my GP. He prescribed a small amount of Valium and suggested I buy one bottle of wine and drink two glasses that day, along with the next, and finish the rest on the third day, just in case I had a withdrawal seizure. My friend drove me to the local shops, feeling odd and not liking the fact I had to continue drinking. I waited until she had gone and started on my first glass of wine. It came straight up, so I continued in true alcoholic fashion to drink the entire bottle and walked to the local shops for more.

She visited me a few mornings. I had held back on my drinking, but she must have known. We were sitting drinking a mug of tea when there was a knock on the door. A medium-sized box arrived, and I announced that it must be the pyjamas I'd ordered. But it was two beautiful thin long-stem vases. I had no recollection of ordering them. She looked puzzled but said nothing.

One morning, my ex-husband rang me and simply said, 'Hear me out.' So I did. He is a wonderful man, who still loves and cares about me, and I feel the same about him. He had researched AA twelve-step rehabs and found one in Worthing. He knew AA had worked for me in the past and asked if I would go for the sake of our kids. I cried and agreed straight away.

My alcoholic madness and delusion was worse when I wasn't drinking, as now I was drinking straight to blackout. I would 'come to' and maybe have the odd thought or feeling but drink it away quickly. Out of respect for my husband and intense love for my children, I managed to stop drinking by reverting to over-the-counter medication

I had a date booked to go to the rehab in Worthing. My kids came and stayed with me for the few days before I was admitted. My ex-husband had emailed and asked me to be 'real' with the kids—no more 'eyes and teeth'. It's a saying one of my best friends and I often used, meaning smiling and looking as though all is well, when in fact, all is far from well. So when the kids arrived, I opened the door and didn't do my usual acting as though I was OK. They could see I wasn't. I had lost a so much weight, had multiple bruises, the worst being across my entire lower back. I'd given up trying to determine how I'd sustained my injuries. I did figure out that my lower back must have resulted from falling down the stairs. I have a beautiful large bowl made out of a single piece of wood that sits at the bottom of the stairs. I noticed it had moved, taken a chunk of plaster out of the wall, and its side shape resembled the bruising on my back. My kids didn't need to say anything, I could see by their faces how upset and terrified they were. I finally let them see the real me—broken, desperate, and so glad to have them with me.

They made no demands on me. We just 'chilled' and did manage to walk to a café in the village for lunch. I was so weak I knew I couldn't manage the walk home, which they understood. We got some groceries in for them, as they were staying on for a few days and caught a taxi home.

My neighbour popped in, and I told her I was going into rehab. I also begged her in front of my kids to keep a very close eye on me when I returned, especially if she saw my heading for the local shops around 8 a.m.

I had to ask my kids to put out my green bags that night for pickup the next day. I wasn't even embarrassed when I showed them the bags. I'd gone past that. They knew the truth. I must admit they did look slightly shocked at the bags lined up against the garage wall. I hadn't put any out for a month, and there must have been at least a hundred bottles, if not more.

My kids offered to come with me on the train from Swansea to Reading. I think their dad had probably said something like, 'Please make sure she gets there.' They handed me over to one of my best friends, who was going to drive me the rest of the way and then caught the next train back to Swansea.

My friend was and always has been amazing—no judgement, just relief that I was safe and about to get help. I had reached a place where I could only stop drinking if I was hospitalised or 'prompted' into rehab.

CHAPTER 6

I AM DONE!

My friend and I arrived at the rehab around 4 p.m. It was a large old house. We were taken into the dining room to fill in forms. My friend left me after I'd answered the preliminary questions, and there I was.

A few clients approached me and offered cups of tea, and I joined them in the garden to smoke. They all seemed lovely, and the staff was very friendly and kind.

I saw the doctor at 5.30 p.m. That meant more questions, but at least I could start a proper detox. My first night was horrendous—sweating, shaking, and a dream that seemed to go all night. In it, there was a loud rooftop party going on above my wardrobe. I asked the partiers to keep the music down, but it got louder. I told them if they passed me a bottle of Champagne down, I would let it go. There was a ladder at the side of my wardrobe. Someone came down and put the Champagne on my dressing table. I staggered out of bed, only to find no Champagne. This went on repeatedly for what seemed like the whole night. I woke up in the morning exhausted, and everything from my dressing table was on the floor—the result of me scrambling time and time again to get the Champagne!

Our days began with meditation at eight. We went around the room giving a one-word 'feelings check'. I struggled to find a word, so it was always *anxious*. A few clients read short readings from various recovery or inspirational books. When asked what we thought about the readings, at least three-quarters of us couldn't remember much about them. The caseworker taking the group smiled and said, 'That's the ISM—incredibly short memory.' I still struggle today but do know generally what I've read in the mornings.

We then listened to soft music, nature sounds, or guided meditation. I found it really hard to concentrate in the beginning, but it got easier. By the end, I loved it. We then had breakfast and showered. The first group was at ten, followed by a short break. Next up was process group run by a therapist between 11 and 12.30. This was a time to talk about any issues, including if you were struggling, thinking about drinking, or using. And it was often very emotional. We had lunch after that, followed by more groups until 5 p.m. During these groups, clients presented twelve-step work and additional work they'd been given. We walked to AA and CA (cocaine anonymous) meetings on Mondays, Tuesdays, Thursdays, and Fridays and had an-in house *Big Book* study on Sunday evenings.

On Thursdays, we had a group after lunch called 'community group'. It was run by a therapist. We were asked if we had any concerns about how things were being run, the food, or anything else. We all received therapeutic duties for the week ahead. Jobs included setting the table for meals, clearing away afterwards, washing up, keeping the outside area clean (which mainly involved brushing up all the cigarette ash), and doing an inventory of the clients' pantry and fridge before ordering what we needed via the chef.

The first week was awful. I was incredibly weak. The detox medication helped, but I needed a few 'top-up' doses to get me through the day. One of the clients was a nurse, absolutely hilarious, and always managed to put a smile on my face. She was presenting her CRP (continued recovery plan) to the group on the day she was leaving. I passed out as I entered the group room. She put me in the recovery position, and I missed her presentation.

We were not allowed to use our mobile phones for the first week, which was fine with me. I really didn't want to talk to anyone. A lovely older part-time therapist ran a group for family and friends on Sundays from 12.30 to 1.30. The friend who took me there and my other best friend came to the session. I don't know what was discussed, but the way they talked and listened to me afterwards was extremely insightful and encouraging. I love the woman who led this group. She has a beautiful aura about her and can give 'the look', as she calls it. I had called myself an arsehole in a group led by her. She peered over her glasses and said, 'That's no way to speak about yourself, young lady.' She was right, but I'd become so used to negative self-talk through my years of drinking, it came naturally. She also referred to the outside world as 'earth land' and talked about how 'earth people' find it difficult to understand our disease. I agree. There is still a lot of judgement around addiction. An impossible belief prevails that we addicts should just be able to stop, which, as we know, is a huge process.

We were allowed out from 1.30 to 4 p.m. on Sundays. My girlfriends visited me every Sunday. We did the same thing every time—walked down to the beach and sat in a tea room, drinking tea and eating an enormous scone with jam and clotted cream. I loved their visits. Being out allowed me to feel 'normal'.

The first piece of written work you are allocated is a brief life story and step one. I found writing my life story hard, especially when it came to describing how my drinking had escalated and all the terrible things I'd done. I sobbed throughout my entire presentation. Your peers do what's called a peer evaluation on you, which involves ticking four potential blocks to recovery and four personal strengths they see in you. They then indicate with ticks whether they think you've accepted your powerlessness and unmanageability. They were useful forms; people often see in you what you cannot see in yourself. I was shocked by some of the blocks that were pointed out to me, but after a while I realised they were very real.

Most of the original group who were there when I arrived left within days of each other. New clients arrived, and by the end of my stay, we became a very close-knit group.

My personal therapist was a lovely younger woman. We met once a week for an hour. She was in recovery, we had a lot in common, and our time together was one of the most beneficial parts of my week. I was so tired and tearful one session. 'Look after your physical body, and your mental/emotional body will follow,' she advised. She was right. I stopped working on my step work for a few days, was allowed some afternoon naps, and ate healthily. I felt much better after a few days.

The manager is a wonderful man. He has a long period of sobriety under his belt and would smoke and chat with us outside. He was so insightful and encouraging. The words of wisdom that came out of his mouth never ceased to amaze me. One morning I told him I was exhausted and really struggling with the daily schedule plus step work. His response was similar to that of AA members in Sydney, which was, 'It may seem hard, but if you put 10 per cent of the effort you put into active addiction into your recovery, there is no reason for you to ever drink again'. He was absolutely right. It made me think of the exhausting, extreme measures I had gone to in order to feed my addiction.

I was given an extra worksheet titled 'Powerlessness'. I felt outraged. I knew I was powerless over alcohol. But as I answered the questions, I realised why I'd been given it. The concept of being powerless over people, places, and things had never truly sunk in. I still liked to control situations and manipulate people. My nephew's wedding, which I'd been uninvited to, was happening halfway through my stay. I was desperately sad and full of shame. One of the male workers asked me to look up page 417 of the *Big Book* and read the section on acceptance. I did and read it out at the start of our meditation the next day:

> Acceptance is the answer to all my problems today. When I am disturbed, it is because I find some person, place, thing or situation—some fact of my life—unacceptable to me, and I can find no serenity until I accept that person, place, thing, or situation as being exactly the way it is supposed to be at this moment.
>
> Nothing, absolutely nothing, happens in God's world by mistake.
>
> Until I could accept my alcoholism, I could not stay sober; unless I accept my life completely on life's terms, I cannot be happy. I need to concentrate not so much on what needs to be changed in the world as on what needs to be changed in me and my attitudes.

It was so true. I believe our amount of acceptance equals our amount of serenity.

My step four was detailed and gave me good insight into my character defects. The problem, I believe, was that I wasn't ready to get rid of them. One day, I arrived early for my session with my therapist. We went outside for a cigarette before the session. She was telling me about an amazing retreat in Greece. It sounded wonderful, and I thought I'd look into going the following year. Once in the session she asked me how I was feeling. I gave my usual answer—anxious. She questioned me further. Two minutes earlier, I had been excited about the idea of the retreat, and now I was saying I felt anxious. She explained that excitement and anxiety can cause the same physical reaction in your body and also suggested I rethink my feeling check-in. She was absolutely right. Morning 'feelings checks' became more real.

One Sunday night, we were upstairs doing the *Big Book* study when we heard crashing and smashing. We thought it was an intruder, but it was, in fact, a seagull who'd managed to get in. He had stuck his beak into all the dinner leftovers, eaten my vegetarian sausage from the clients' kitchen bin, flown around the living room pooing on the furniture, and finally regurgitated my sausage behind one of the couches. We laughed for days, wondering how he'd got in, and started saying, 'Maybe he came in the back door.' This led to lots of hilarious sexual innuendoes! We named the seagull Cedric and were sure it was him sitting on the fence outside the clients' kitchen window in the days that followed.

On the day you leave you present to the group and therapists your CRP. I'd spent hours on mine and was determined to stick to it. I presented it. After each presentation, a key ring is passed around. Everyone gives you feedback and says nice things about you, filling the key ring with love and good wishes. I felt nervous leaving and was dreading walking back into my home—the crime scene, as I called it.

On the train ride to Swansea, within an hour, I was thinking about how the buffet cart sold wine. *Really?* I had just spent five weeks in rehab. I prayed the thought away and arrived home safely.

The sponsor I already had was good. She encouraged me to go to as many meetings as I could and met up with me once a week to see how I was doing. I worked through steps one, two, and three during the first month. I went straight back to the drug and alcohol centre. My first time was a Friday, which was band practice. It turned out the group had kept bringing the keyboard out every Friday in the hope I would return.

I suffered chronic anxiety. It was worse in the mornings, and I couldn't speak to anyone before 10 a.m., not even my best friends. It had been agreed that I would phone them rather than text, which was totally reasonable. Texting had been a major feat, requiring, firstly, more booze to gain courage and, secondly, attempts to text a few coherent lines while even more drunk. I would later learn that my friends, kids, and others always knew I was drunk when they received them.

I went to stay with my friend who had taken me to rehab and her family in Tunbridge Wells. I was up front about my anxiety. Everyone in her family, especially her youngest daughter, who has incredible insight for a seventeen-year-old, was wonderful. I had a lovely four days. My friend and her family put no demands on me and simply allowed me to chill and be part of the family.

A lovely Christian counsellor had been arranged by the managers of the Christian retreat. Our sessions focused mainly on the dynamics of my family. On her fourth visit, she wrote me a 'prescription'. Puzzled, I stared at the piece of paper. On it said, 'I am enough. I am enough just as I am. I am enough because God made me.' Tears poured down my face as I realised how much I hated myself and the fact my loved one's had suffered so much as a result of my alcoholism. I did as she suggested which was read it three times a day. I cried each time I read it. The only hope I clung onto was the truth that 'I am enough because God made me.' This was to become my biggest encouragement during the months of chaos awaiting me.

I felt particularly positive one morning and was almost marching, head held high, feeling rather like Bridget Jones walking across London Bridge the night after she'd shagged Hugh Grant. I was plugged into my 'Recovery Playlist'. 'Never Give Up on a Good Thing', by George Benson was playing as I arrived at my least favourite meeting. An older woman went first. 'I'm having a fucking awful day,' she began. 'My Hoover broke this morning, so I kicked the fucker. And I've got to look after my fucking grandchildren this afternoon.' *Wow*—not exactly carrying the message of hope and strength. After others shared, I looked at them and thought, *You'd be better off drinking if you're that miserable.* This was so unjust of me, as the only requirement for membership in AA is a desire to stop drinking.

I was standing at the bus stop waiting to catch my bus to the personal development group. A woman started talking to me. She went on and on, and it was all I could do not to tell her to shut up. I was still full of anxiety. I found bus rides challenging and feared anyone talking to me, let alone sitting next to me. I shared this with the group, and it led to a discussion about how we perceive people and how the way people look is not necessarily a reflection of how they feel inside. That was true for me. I had no idea how this woman had been feeling. Maybe she was lonely? Maybe a parent had died?

During one of these personal development sessions, a new client sat opposite me. She thought I was a member of the staff. This wasn't an isolated incident. It happened with a few other clients, and while in rehab, a few visitors also mistook me for a member of staff. That's how good I am at pretending and acting. In fact I, along with many other addicts, could probably win an Oscar for our performances.

In early September, my son came to stay for ten days. He was between flats and had been working ten-hour days at the Fringe Festival in Edinburgh. We had a lovely time chilling out and watching films. Plus, we went to our favourite vegetarian café in the village for lunch a few times. I had anxiety over what we would eat in the evenings. My son looked in my freezer and food cupboards and said, 'Mum, we have enough food here for a month.' We shopped locally for fresh produce. It was as though he was the parent and I was the child.

The drug and alcohol centre was putting on an end-of-summer barbecue, and the band was going to be playing. My son came with me. I was nervous, as I hadn't practised much. So I kept the volume down low. He signalled to me 'turn it up' and kept giving me the thumbs up. Our gig ended after three songs. I found out later the lead singer had a panic attack and so couldn't carry on. Plus, it began to rain.

I had noticed my son talking to the lovely man who plays the bass and rarely talks and asked him what they'd been talking about. He said 'stuff' and the bass guitar, which my son also plays. I felt so proud of him, the way he mixed and chatted with everyone there.

The only AA meeting I could walk to was on Saturday evenings. During his stay, I went to the meeting and they asked if anybody would like to volunteer as an additional tea and coffee person. My hand shot up, as I truly believed, 'This is it. I'll never drink again'.

After he left, I felt lonely, and began to isolate. I forced myself to go to the Saturday meeting, armed with biscuits and milk as I'd made this commitment the previous week. It wasn't long before I was drinking again, so no additional tea and coffee person for the Saturday night meeting. I was too ashamed to ring any of the lovely ladies who had given me their phone numbers, so I simply vanished without a trace.

My girlfriends became suspicious, as I was texting, not ringing. And when I did speak to one of them on a Saturday morning, I was slurring my speech and said I was just tired. I came to on the kitchen floor later that day. I had excruciating pain in my right shoulder so drank to get rid of the pain. Both my girlfriends knew I was drinking so phoned the rehab to see if a bed was available. Thankfully, a spot was open for the following day. One of my friends has an older sister who lives near me. She rang her and asked her to come over and help me pack. My shoulder was incredibly painful, and she kept saying we needed to go to hospital. I refused, and she helped me pack. I knew I was incapable of getting a train the following morning, so she rang a local car agency and booked a driver to pick me up at 8 a.m. the next day. She asked if I had any wine left in the house. I lied and said no. After she left, I carried on drinking but barely slept. I was terrified of oversleeping.

The driver arrived bang on time. He was lovely and a smoker, which was a bonus. We stopped at two service stations on the journey. I texted my kids and told them I was going in for relapse prevention. I couldn't bear hurting them anymore. I also texted my friend from church who was friendly with my Mum and asked her to lie for me. I rang one of my best friends on the journey and told her what I'd done. She agreed I'd done the right thing, as Mum particularly didn't need any more stress.

CHAPTER 7

THIS IS IT ...

I arrived around midday. One of the benefits of going back to the same place was that the staff knew me. Plus I knew the daily and weekly routines. When I met with the doctor, I totally forgot to mention my shoulder. I was dazed and just wanted to start my detox. I locked my door on the first night. I've no idea why I did this, as I had never done it before. In the morning, I was wearing my towel and headed for the shower. I'd forgotten my soap and realised I was locked out. I crept down, clutching my towel. A male caseworker took one look at my shoulder and asked me what had happened. It was covered in bruises that stretched down my back, and my entire right boob was turning black. He organised for me to see the doctor later that day. The pain was unbearable, and all I could take was Ibuprofen. I couldn't lift my arm up at all. I managed to shower but stopped at washing my hair. That would be too difficult.

Later that day, a different male caseworker took me to the local doctor's surgery. He came in with me, which made me feel less nervous. The doctor prescribed Co-codamol, which was highly unusual at the rehab, as it contains codeine. He also said I needed an X-ray, which was done the following morning. I was nervous about being on this painkiller, given my history of codeine abuse. But I needed it for the pain, especially in the morning before my shower. I managed to wash my hair that morning. It took ages and made me think how I'd always taken for granted the use of my right arm.

It was a beautiful day, so the same worker and I walked to the hospital. I was X-rayed within half an hour of our arrival. Shortly after that, the radiographer came up and said there was a fracture and I may need pins or plates. I burst into tears as we were shown to a small waiting room. I went straight outside for a cigarette and returned, still crying. The caseworker, who has been sober for a long time and works a very tight AA/NA programme, was just the person I needed to sit and listen to my alcoholic madness. I was starting to sweat and needed my detox medication, which he arranged straight away with a nurse. Numerous cigarettes and an hour later, I still hadn't been seen. I was going crazy thinking how much I didn't want surgery. It would mean being in hospital and missing valuable time in rehab. I was sobbing and watching the clock. Knowing I was suffering and quite crazy, he suggested, 'How about you say the Serenity Prayer'?

I shut my eyes and repeated the prayer four times quickly in my head. Then I turned to him and said, 'It's not fucking working.'

I was due painkillers, which he managed to get from the nurse. We were finally called back to the X-ray department. I saw a doctor, who had looked at the X-ray, and was so relieved when she said I'd spilt my clavicle (collarbone) but wouldn't need surgery. A temporary sling was put on, and I was given an appointment to return in two weeks for review and a more permanent sling.

We walked back to the rehab, and I said I was too exhausted to go to the CA meeting that night. I'd tried to get out of a meeting during the third day of my first admission. Now I was asking the same caseworker again. He said, 'Come on, kiddo. I know you're in pain, but a meeting would really help you tonight.'

He was right. The meeting was great, and I managed to get some, though not much, broken sleep.

I was incapable of doing any washing up or any of the therapeutic duties other than the shopping list twice a week. I felt guilty and kept apologising to the other clients. One morning I was in the kitchen apologising again. The caseworker who'd sat with me and my madness in hospital was in there. 'Why do you keep apologising?' he asked. 'You washed up all the time when you were here last time.' He was right. I'd done other people's jobs many times. My chronic people-pleasing had been in full flight.

I was allocated a different therapist this admission, as my previous therapist had left. This new counsellor was the senior therapist, and seeing him worked out really well. He had years of recovery and could see straight through me. And as they say, 'You can't bullshit a bullshitter.'

My life story and step one were almost identical to my first presentation of these things. The only additions were more blackout falls, one of which had resulted in a fractured clavicle.

I was given extra work—a self-esteem worksheet. I'd managed to dodge it last time but had seen how my nurse friend struggled with hers. One of the questions instructed, 'Name five things you like about your appearance.' I looked at myself in the mirror and just saw a broken person who had no self-esteem or sense of worth. The other clients were really helpful and started saying all the nice things they could see. Some of the men went for boobs and so forth!

One of my best friends was working in Spain for six weeks and therefore unable to visit. My other best friend visited. She had always been and still was level-headed and logical. We went out one Sunday for our usual cream tea, and I told her about the self-esteem sheet. She smiled and said, 'Think about all the things you've achieved in your life—a brilliant nurse, a fantastic mum, and an extremely supportive corporate wife.' We talked about out inter-railing around Europe, the fact I'd been on the netball and hockey teams, and the list went on. I was so grateful for the way she, along with my other best friends, had always encouraged me. When I got back, I filled in the whole sheet. I had accomplished and overcome many things before I'd crossed the line into full-blown alcoholism. The following Sunday, my friend came with her husband. Another cream tea and again it was lovely to be out in 'earth land'.

When I delivered the self-esteem sheet to the group and therapist, I was tearful thinking of all those years I'd lost to drinking. What had happened to the fun-loving, adventurous, caring, and loving me? The feedback from my peers was so lovely. A lot of them said, 'We wish you could see in yourself what we all see in you.'

The therapist asked me to say out loud, 'I love myself.' That was far too much of a stretch. But I was able to shout, '*I like myself.*' I didn't really like myself at all, but did what I was told—that's me, anything to please people!

A man arrived in shortly after me. He was in for alcohol and serious codeine addiction. The detox medication made him very drowsy, but we hit it off from the start. He had a great sense of humour. We laughed all the time we were together, and he became my 'bestie'.

He had a wonderful beard. I could tell he looked after it, as it was perfectly manicured. One morning, he was trimming it with clippers when a worker knocked on his door. He jumped and took a large chunk out of the left side. He was mortified but took it in good humour, and we all kept telling him (truthfully) that it was barely noticeable and would grow back quickly. We did a shameful yet unintentional thing one day. The next-door building was a home for mentally ill people. There was a man whose window overlooked at the spot where we would smoke outside; he spent his days licking his windows. My friend popped his head over the wall and said, 'How are things, mate?'

The man replied with the question of his own. 'Are you the ones who take drugs and drink too much?'

I popped my head up, and we both said, 'Yes, that's us' and gave him a thumbs up.

Poor chap went into some sort of psychotic rage. We heard the staff in his room, and then there was silence. He must have been sedated. We had no idea our behaviour would cause such an extreme reaction.

My bestie, who was still on heavy detox meds, decided one evening he would ride side saddle down the bannister. I tried to stop him, but he was determined to do it. He'd made it barely a fourth of the way down when he shot off and banged into the wall. He looked dazed but insisted he could do it and wanted to try again. I suggested coffee and a cigarette might be a better option, which he agreed to. So I helped him outside. We smoked two cigarettes, one after the other. He was still adamant that at a second attempt would be successful. It took all my persuasion, several more cigarettes, and trips by me to the kitchen to make more coffee to convince him otherwise.

We invented the 'Recovery Song and Dance'. We would sing, 'We deserve recovery, recovery, recovery. We deserve recovery.' And we had a jig to go with it. It caught on with some of our peers. And light-hearted though it may have been, the message of our song was true. We all deserved recovery.

During one of our Sunday-night in-house *Big Book* study sessions, which were led by the lovely caseworker who'd sat with me after my X-ray, he gave us all a handout. On the front page was the arch of freedom, which explained how step one was the foundation, step two was the cornerstone (belief through hope), step three was the keystone (direction through the decision to turn our will and lives over to a loving God), and steps four through to nine spoke to freedom through action. The second page described the first three steps:

- In step one, we have a physical allergy and mental obsession and lack power.
- In step two, we have fellowship supports and experience spiritual changes, which equals power.
- Step three, decision, is the turning point, and we can go one of two ways. Firstly, we can disbelieve and continue to drink, risking insanity or death. Or secondly, we can believe and accept spiritual help, which leads to sanity and sobriety.

This is so true. I've tested it enough times to know that the steps really do work, if done properly and truthfully. The idea of having a physical allergy to alcohol made sense for the first time. If I had an allergy to nuts or seafood, I would simply not eat them.

I had told all the staff members about my lie about being in for relapse prevention. A male caseworker came out with an absolute gem. 'If you don't tell a lie, you will never have to remember.' How true. I'd told so many lies and got so confused about what was actually real. Lies to cover up lies, then more lies—it was absolutely exhausting!

We each made a personal shopping list on Mondays and Thursdays. The list would include things like cigarettes, toiletries, and so on, and we got the items we'd requested the following day. I went in to get mine one Friday. Even as a smoker, I couldn't believe the amount of cigarette packets that were lined up on one of the desks—different brands, different amounts. I looked at them and felt like pushing them into the centre of the table and saying, 'All in.'

I'll recap my style of 'gambling'. I've gambled with my life more times than I could possibly know. Jails, institutions, and death were among the very real stakes talked about in AA. I attended AA funerals in Sydney—beautiful people whom I'd got to know. I've also known of many others who have died, most of whom killed themselves while drunk, and others did so during extreme 'dry drunk' times. I have a big fat tick next to institutions, and it is only by the Grace of God that I'm alive and did not end up in jail.

Saturday afternoons were free time with an optional walk with a member of staff. I always chose to stay behind, as I needed some alone time. I had a sleep one Saturday and woke up at 4 p.m. to find a document had been slipped under my door. It was a worksheet entitled 'Perfectionism'.

I was groggy and pissed off, as I had never thought of myself as a perfectionist. I marched up to the therapist's office, banged on the door, and waved the sheet at my therapist. I told him I didn't have time to do it properly and didn't think I was a perfectionist.

He stopped my ranting with a smile and asked, 'Have you read the questions yet?'

I hadn't, which was, as it turns out, the very reason he'd given it to me. My step work was always well put together. I behaved like the 'perfect' client—never breaking a rule and always being polite and helpful.

I was still angry about having to do the assignment, so I marched downstairs into the office and said to the worker who'd told me the great line about not lying meaning you didn't have to remember. 'I was thinking of asking you for some Co-codamol,' I said.

He smiled and said, 'I wouldn't have given it to you even if you had.'

This is my problem. Drink and drugs aren't my problem—*I am*. When things don't go my way, I'm upset, resentful, and carry other negative feelings. I medicate my feelings and thoughts away. When I looked at the questions on the perfectionism worksheet, this made total sense. As I answered the questions, I realised that, since I'd been a young girl, I had always tried to make people happy—be the perfect child, sister, wife, mum, and friend.

In our next one-hour session, my therapist asked me about my childhood. I explained that I had truly believed as a young girl that my role was to try and keep the family happy. *That wasn't my job.* I had always put high expectations on myself and others, so the worksheet was a huge turning point in my recovery. I didn't have to be 'perfect' at anything. No one is perfect. All I needed to do was work on my recovery, stay sober, and cause no more harm to my loved ones. My final session revolved around my loneliness, and the need to let go of the dream that I would grow old with my first husband. I'd buried the pain and disappointment; these were things he decided to start working on.

There was a young man who'd been there since I'd arrived. He was disruptive in group, wasn't taking it seriously, and had already been given two warnings. One was for throwing the cat across the sitting room at a client, and the other was for constantly commenting on my bestie's eyebrows and saying he had 'staring eyes'. The three of us were out smoking one morning when he turned to me and whispered, 'I've also wondered what a fifty-year-old women's arse feels like.' I dismissed his comment and started to walk inside. He grabbed both my cheeks—worse than that, his hands were right between my legs as he grabbed me. I was so shocked, I said nothing. He did it again once we were inside the door and then followed me into the clients' kitchen. We were alone, and he said, 'I'd like to check out the rest of you.' With that, he grabbed me around my waist and brushed against my boobs. Again I was too shocked to say anything.

I finally told the staff, who took it very seriously. Thankfully, my bestie had witnessed the bottom groping, and we were called up to see the manager. He asked if I'd like to get the police involved. I said no. I didn't want the distraction of being interviewed, so he said he would speak with his manager and keep me updated.

I was called up to his office again, and he explained the man would need to be reported to a certain organisation, which would result in him possibly finding it hard to get a job. I agreed to that. He said the man would be discharged and that it would happen while I was out having my follow-up appointment with the orthopaedic doctor. A female worker who knew me well took me to my appointment; my temporary sling had stretched, and my arm was lying far too low down. The consultant looked shocked at the sling's situation, and I was given a heavy-duty sling, which felt much more comfortable. The worker phoned the rehab to make sure the man had left. He had, so we walked home.

A fabulous gay guy arrived back in. He'd been in for two weeks, gone on a cruise with his auntie, and come back for his last two weeks. He was so much fun, and very in touch with his feminine side. I'm pretty vain, and told him I was concerned my fingers were getting stained from the cigarettes. He skipped off and returned with a peg from the washing line. *Genius*, I thought. From then on, I was known as peg lady. He loved the recovery song and dance and, on the day he was leaving, asked if he could go in my room. He wrote in big red marker, 'You deserve recovery. Kisses and hearts.' I looked at it every day.

It was my son's birthday while I was in. I texted him in the morning and arranged a time for us to speak later. I sang 'Happy Birthday' very badly through the phone, and we had a lovely conversation. My kids have been and still are amazing with me. They love me unconditionally and encourage me endlessly, and all they want is to see me well and happy. I loved my phone calls with them. The two of them are so different. My daughter would always start by saying, 'Are you having fun?' as if I were on vacation. She always asked about the food, which was great; the chef made me lovely vegetarian meals. My son would always say how much he loved me, as did my daughter. Every phone call he would say, 'I really hope you're not beating yourself up emotionally.'

I realised I'd been taking the Co-codamol for two weeks and thought I should start reducing it. I wanted to be off it for at least a week to ten days before I went home. Being an all-or-nothing addict, I made up my own reducing regime. I decided to just take it in the mornings before I showered and at bedtime. This backfired. I sat in agony, having refused the 6 p.m. dose, in an AA meeting. I barely heard a word, and the staff sat me down and said, 'You are on these for a valid reason. How about just missing the lunchtime dose?'

I followed that suggestion for two days. Ibuprofen and paracetamol worked well together, so I substituted my lunchtime and 6 p.m. dose with these. It was painful, but I wanted to get off the heavier painkillers. I was finally off them after three weeks. The pain was still bad but not unbearable.

There was another woman in with the same name as me. Our surnames began with G and T, not ideal given we were both in for alcohol. We all found her very annoying; she was negative the entire time she was there. What really pissed me off was that she kept crying and saying, 'I can't believe how low you've gone and all the terrible things you've done. My partner loves me so much and writes me notes every day.' *Great*! As if I didn't feel enough shame over what I had done during my drinking and blackouts.

She spent hours on her life story, and asked if she could read it out to me. I don't know why I agreed, but after hearing it, I said, 'I'm sorry you had to go through all that.'

She burst into tears and said, 'I thought you'd be more shocked.'

I wasn't. I'd heard far worse, and as she kept reminding me, my journey was so much worse than hers. She called me insensitive, which was absolutely not the case. It was during this admission I learnt the importance of 'keeping myself safe'—this included not allowing myself to get sucked into others dramas. I'd done this in the extreme during my first recovery, and at times it proved extremely detrimental to my own emotional sobriety.

I spent a lot of time on my step four and presented step five to the group and the lovely older therapist who ran the family and friends sessions. She had heard my previous step five and said she had never heard such honesty from me. My thinking, feelings, and behaviours towards others had a common thread. They all involved my false pride—feeling better or less than (I'd spent most of my life feeling less than)—dishonesty, envy, selfishness, shame, and fear. Fear underpins all my character defects. I can still be fearful today. I fear relapsing if I don't do everything I need to do on a daily basis to remain clean and sober.

The same lady was running 'process group'. We started with the usual one-word feeling check, and mine was *mischievous*. She was a firm believer in the 'inner child' concept and the importance of treating yourself with the love and care you deserve. She asked me to say a bit more about my feeling *mischievous*. I said 'little me' was out to play. She asked me if I thought it was a healthy feeling. I immediately said yes but soon realised that, while having fun was good, I needed to reign myself in before I got 'too playful', which would take my focus off my recovery. I believe humour and laughter are wonderful gifts from God, especially in rehab and once at home as well. I had barely laughed at all during the past twenty months. Laughter is healing and infectious. There were many times someone would say or do something funny, and our laughter could be heard by the staff inside.

It was getting close to my discharge date. The manager and my therapist both urged me stay an extra week, but I refused, believing I could do this.

I presented my CRP, again very detailed. The key ring was passed around, and I said my goodbyes to my peers. Most people say, 'I know you'll make it' or 'I've every faith in you.' I don't say that when people are leaving, as there is no guarantee any of us will 'make it'. Statistics show the success rate is between 5 and 10 per cent, which is extremely low. I comment on their CRP. If it's good, I say, 'If you do everything on this plan, there's no reason why you should pick up a drink or drug again.'

My therapist did my discharge paperwork with me, and when one of my best friends picked me up, his parting words were, 'Be wise. No more tap dancing. Be wise.'

When I got home I was exhausted. My shoulder was still very sore, and I began taking large amounts of Codeine-based painkillers. I went to a few meetings in the first week and back to the drug and alcohol centre.

I woke up one morning and thought a glass of wine would help with the pain. It's never *a* glass of wine with me. So there I was, drinking three bottles of wine a day again. One Friday, I had drunk two bottles of wine by 9 a.m. I couldn't go back to sleep so took about ten Valium tablets. I don't know if I rang my minister or my friend who's friendly with my Mum first. My friend arrived and drove me to hospital. I lay across the seat. I know she was terrified and praying the whole way there.

We arrived at the hospital, and I was seen by a nurse straight away. We then sat in a small waiting room for what seemed like hours. Finally a doctor came and ordered blood tests, including one to test my liver function, and we waited another few hours for the results. I was dizzy but desperate for a cigarette, so my friend helped me outside. I texted my sponsor and told her what had happened. She said she would be at my place by 6.30 p.m.

My blood work came back normal, and I was told we could leave. As we were walking towards the car, we spotted our minister, who had driven all the way there to see if we were both OK. I hugged him and cried. He prayed for us both and thanked God that I was OK—another miracle, absolutely.

My friend dropped me off, and my sponsor arrived and stayed with me for a few hours. She'd planned on staying the night, but I said I would be fine and just wanted to go to bed. I left it ten minutes after she left and then went straight to the local shops to buy more wine.

As my battle continued, it seemed as though my all consuming need to drink far outweighed any potentially life-threatening consequences. This may sound as though I'd lost the will to live, which was definitely not the case. I thank God that in the midst of all the chaos he gave me glimpse after glimpse of hope.

So many baffling things happened once I was drinking to blackout. I said I never ate while drinking, which is true. But I woke up one morning to an awful smell. I'd ordered Chinese take-away, enough for a family, £64 worth! I must have opened it to have a look and left it strewn over the breakfast bar. Then followed the cunning part. Feeling ashamed, I scooped it up and put it straight into the outside bin—heaven forbid anyone should know! As for powerful part, all I can say is, God willing, I'll never underestimate the power of addiction.

My friend rang me from Spain. She could hear in my voice I'd been drinking but said nothing about it. Later that day, unbeknown to me, my friends had discussed what to do. They'd rung the rehab, and there was a bed available the next day. I agreed to go, as I knew I couldn't stop. I stood a good chance of more blackout falls that could prove fatal.

I slowed my drinking down in order to pack and managed to book a train from Swansea to Reading, leaving at 8.30 a.m. the following day. I drank myself to sleep and woke up feeling groggy but ready to go. A taxi arrived at 7.30, and I was just about to get in when I saw my neighbours. I sobbed and told them what had happened. They were lovely and wished me well. I arrived at the station at 7.50, dragged my case across the road to a small supermarket, and tried to buy a bottle of wine, only to be told the shop couldn't sell it until 8. I dragged my case back, had a cigarette, and returned and bought two bottles of wine. I went into the toilets and swigged about half a bottle.

I had a window seat, thankfully with no one beside me, so I drank the wine within the first half hour. I needed more so went to the buffet cart and bought a three-quarter-sized bottle, which I drank straight away.

My friend who was in Spain rang me at some point during the journey. I have no recollection of the conversation, and she later told me she'd never heard me that drunk. Thankfully I'd set the alarm on my phone for five minutes before I was due to arrive at Reading station. I have no idea how I managed to get off the train but vaguely remember two men talking to me in a waiting room. My phone was ringing. They answered it. It was my friend. They said I kept saying I wanted to get a taxi to Worthing and asked her if I was good for the money. She said yes and explained I was going to rehab. The taxi driver looked concerned and asked if I was going to vomit in his taxi. I said no, and he let me lay across the back seat until we arrived at the rehab centre.

CHAPTER 8

DESPERATION

It had only been sixteen days since I'd left the rehab centre. I stumbled through the doors drunk, dazed, and thinking, *How the hell did I get back to this place?* I blew way over on the breathalyser, so had to wait for six hours before I could start my detox medication. The lovely nurse was in. I was so glad to see her. We hugged and I cried.

There was a lovely lady about my age who soon became my 'bestie' this time around. My first day was all a bit of a blank. I have naturally low blood pressure and fainted twice. The second day was better. I was still dizzy, as the meds had kicked in. My new bestie helped me walk to the AA meeting in the evening. She was wonderful. I had to keep stopping and hold onto walls, but I made it there with her help.

As I said before, the advantage of returning to the same place was the familiarity, which made it easier. The staff welcomed me back, and I was allocated the same therapist. The first week was OK. The staff had allowed me to do my life story and step one during my second week, which was a blessing.

The female worker who had taken me to get my new sling looked me in the eyes one morning and said, 'I've never seen you this low. There's not even the flicker of a flame in your eyes.' She also suggested that maybe, subconsciously, I kept coming back because I knew it was a safe place. She could well have been right.

The AA promises, found in pages 83–84 in the *Big Book*, were posted on a ground-floor wall, directly opposite the staircase. I'd memorised them during my first recovery, but their meaning sank in deeper as I sat daily on the bottom stair waiting for medication or to speak with a member of staff. In fact, I would often just sit and stare at them, tearful and desperately wanting to believe them. They read as follows:

1. If we are painstaking about this phase of our development, we will be amazed before we are half way through.
2. We are going to know a new freedom and a new happiness.
3. We will not regret the past nor wish to shut the door on it.
4. We will comprehend the word serenity and we will know peace.
5. No matter how far down the scale we have gone, we will see how our experience can benefit others.
6. That feeling of uselessness and self-pity will disappear.
7. We will lose interest in selfish things and gain interest in our fellows.
8. Self-seeking will slip away.
9. Our whole attitude and outlook upon life will change.
10. Fear of people and of economic insecurity will leave us.
11. We will intuitively know how to handle situations which used to baffle us.
12. We will suddenly realise that God is doing for us what we could not do for ourselves.

Are these extravagant promises? We think not. They are being fulfilled among us-sometimes quickly, sometimes slowly. They will always materialise if we work for them.

During this admission, I finally re-grasped the incredible hope recovery holds and actually believed these amazing promises could, over time, come true.

My nurse friend left at the beginning of my second week. She knew if she relapsed again, she would lose joint custody of her daughter, whom she adored. She texted me every day and rang the rehab to say she was OK. On the Friday, I knew her daughter was coming to stay with her, so I sent her a text, saying, 'Enjoy the cuddles' and adding a smiley face. I didn't hear back from her that night, which was fine. I imagined she was having a wonderful time.

We were allowed to use our phones from lunchtime onwards at the weekends. It was Saturday afternoon, and I was about to phone my kids but saw a text message from her saying, 'It's got me.' I had a pretty good idea what she meant but texted her back anyway, saying, 'Do you mean the booze?' I told her I was there for her and that I loved her.

At my first session with my therapist, I told him about the text. He asked what I thought I should do in order to keep myself safe. Good question. I knew the answer but felt guilty about it. I needed to text her back and say I needed to cease all contact until she was sober in order to protect myself. After the session, I saw a missed call from her and listened to the voicemail. She was drunk and desperately wanted me to ring her. I went to speak to the caseworker, the same one who had told me those memorable words— 'If you don't tell a lie, you'll never have to remember.' He sat looking at me and said almost exactly what my therapist had said. I texted her the reason I couldn't have any contact with her. I was in my room having just spoken to my kids when I saw another missed call from her, and there was another voicemail. I hadn't thought to block her number. The voicemail was heartbreaking, so I texted her and advised she reach out for help, but not to me.

My friend was back from Spain. She texted me and asked if she could visit me with her new partner. I said absolutely. After I'd sent my reply I thought, *What an awful way to meet him for the first time, me in rehab.*

We had a lovely few hours out, enjoying the cream tea as usual. And he was incredible. He asked me what we did each day and was genuinely caring. I'd never seen my friend look so relaxed and in love. It was wonderful. The following Sunday she visited with her daughter. We shared another trip to the tea rooms and a lovely few hours. It always felt so nice to get out for a few hours and hear about life outside rehab.

I presented my life story and step one again to the group and therapist. I was tearful as I read out all my near-death experiences and had to stop a few times. I knew with all my being I was totally powerless over alcohol and that the unmanageability had become increasingly dangerous. My peer evaluations were spot on. I had too many concerns outside group. I was a perfectionist. I was struggling and was at risk of old behaviour, which would lead me back to drinking.

A lovely man was in for cocaine addiction. His marriage was on the rocks, and he was facing the possibility of losing custody of his daughter, who he loved dearly. He and I became pantry pals. We would often be in there guzzling chocolate biscuits and bars. We would always have a morning cuddle in the pantry. There was nothing sinister in this. We simply enjoyed a cuddle. I gave most of my peers a morning cuddle but always asked new arrivals if they would like a cuddle. I had lacked intimacy and hugs for a long time, so I loved the morning hugs. My bestie and I were always up around 5 a.m., smoking together outside and desperate for the night staff to wake up so we could make ourselves a mug of tea. This happened at 6.45 a.m. She and I shared so many hugs and laughs during our stay. She had brought herself some thin Christmas slippers when she was out with her sons the previous Sunday. The end of her cigarette fell into her sleeve. She flicked it off, and it landed on her highly flammable slippers. She bent over to put it out and let out the longest fart I'd heard in years. I loved her brazenness. She wasn't ashamed to fart. It happened on numerous occasions and made everyone laugh.

There was always a mystery around what happened to the abundance of cigarette lighters, which seemed to disappear on a daily basis. I likened it to the 'sock monster' when my kids were growing up. I never fathomed out why, despite my methodical laundry regime, there would nearly always be one missing. I had woken up at 4.30 one morning and realised I had no lighter—disaster! Thankfully my 'bestie' was up at five, which saved the day. I was sitting in the garden later that day with a few of my peers and told them of my awful start to the day and then announced, 'There's nothing worse than finding yourself without a lighter at 4 a.m.'

One chuckled and said, 'Think about that—are you sure there's nothing worse?'

He was absolutely right. This was what AA would call a quality problem. Of course far worse things had happened to me, to the point of nearly dying. This comment was another crucial turning point in my recovery, coupled with gratitude. I no longer need worry, let alone become anxious over small annoyances.

I loved the music and art sessions, which had been introduced a few months previously to the weekly schedule. In music, there would be a topic, for example, hope or fear. We would each pick a song that meant something to us. During my second admission, I'd chosen Abba's 'Dancing Queen'. I sobbed throughout the entire song, as it reminded me of how I had danced with my daughter so many times while we watched *Mamma Mia!* I longed to dance with her again. One time, I chose a song called 'Beautiful Mess', by Jason Mraz, which, for me, depicted the final years of my time with my first husband. The sessions were often very emotional, but there were many happy songs that put all of us in a good mood. Art therapy was fun. I'm no artist. Stick figure drawings are about my limit. Some of my peers, on the other hand, drew meaningful masterpieces. The therapist asked us to explain our artwork, and he always saw far more in it than we did.

Christmas was only a month away, and both kids were coming to stay. My son phoned me one Saturday night and said, 'Please, Mum, don't do your usual manic cooking and freezing of food before we come, and please leave the tree for us to decorate.' I admired his honesty and told him so. Freezing food and pre-decorating the tree was exactly what I would have done in the past.

My step two should have been easy, but I struggled in prayer every morning. It was all I could do to say the Serenity Prayer:

> God grant me the serenity to accept the things I cannot change, the courage to change the things I can, and the wisdom to know the difference.

On a good day, I managed to say the 'Third Step Prayer':

> God, I offer myself to thee—to build with me and to do with me as thou will. Relieve me of the bondage of self, that I may better do thy will. Take away my difficulties, that victory over them may bear witness to those I would help of thy power, thy love, and thy way of life. May I do thy will always.

Saying 'Always' felt like an impossible task. I am human after all, and I knew my perfectionism had complicated my life considerably. So I decided to change the ending to 'May I do your will to the best of my ability.' Maybe this was a cop-out, but it seems to be working now.

I had a beautiful yet disturbing dream one night. My Dad was lying next to me stroking my hair, hugging me softly, and saying, 'Come on, Daught, you can beat this'. I woke up expecting him to be there. Obviously, he wasn't. I tried desperately to fall asleep and be with him again but couldn't. It was 4 a.m. I went outside and smoked two cigarettes, cried in my room, and decided to do some journaling.

At the start of my third week, my morning prayer time was still hard. One morning at 5 a.m., I lay on the bed, arms stretched out, and cried out to God, 'Why am I not being set free?'

I didn't feel much, just tiredness. But I texted my friend from church that evening and told her how I was struggling. I knew that she, along with the Monday Girls (a group of ladies including my mum), my minister, and many others had been praying for so long for this to happen. She replied and simply said, 'Have faith.'

My prayer time became easier. I'd taken a small Bible in with me and read some of my favourite bits of it every morning. I have a fridge magnet, which my mum gave me years ago. It says, 'Be still and know that I am God' (Psalm 46:19). I also have a bookmark on which is written the well-known story called 'Footprints in the Sand':

> One night, a man had a dream. He dreamed he was walking along the beach with the Lord.
>
> Across the sky flashed scenes from his life. For each scene, he noticed two sets of footprints in the sand; one belonged to him and the other to the Lord.
>
> When the last scene of his life flashed before him, he looked back at the footprints in the sand. He noticed that many times along the path of his life, there was only one set of footprints. He also noticed that it happened at the very lowest and saddest times in his life.
>
> This really bothered him and he questioned the Lord about it. 'Lord, you said that once I decided to follow you, you'd walk with me all the way. But I have noticed that during the most troublesome times in my life, there is only one set of footprints. I don't understand why when I needed you most you would leave me.'

The Lord replied, 'My precious, precious child, I love you and would never leave you. During those times of trial and suffering, when you see only one set of footprints, it was then that I carried you.'

I love this story. As I look back across my life, I know that God has carried me through so many dangers and times of suffering, sadness, grief, and desperation. I believe nothing, absolutely nothing, is wasted in God's plans and that, if I stay connected to him, I will be safe and free from fear and ultimately become the woman he intended me to be. Not that I know what that entails yet, but it's a wonderful assurance that I need never go backwards.

The manager, as I said before, often chatted with us outside while we smoked, and there were always words of wisdom. One morning, I was outside with my bestie. We were chatting with the manager, and he was talking about the importance of keeping it in the day or hour if necessary. He told us a funny story about himself in early recovery. He called it his 'time travel suit', which was silver with a helmet to match. He described how his mind would wander (time travel) and how difficult it was for him to keep it in the day. We laughed so much, as my bestie could picture him in his silver suit and helmet. He also came out with a comment regarding addicts ('busted, disgusted, and not to be trusted') that resonated. That was me; I had been busted on so many occasions, disgusted with myself, and most definitely not to be trusted. The first time travel comment made me think. I'd never really kept it in the day and wasn't doing it while in there. I was thinking ahead about Christmas and what I would cook and buy for my kids. I needed to stay focussed and not miss a minute during this third admission.

A woman came in who'd been at the centre six months earlier. She arrived drunk, was loud, and staggered around saying she knew the drill. Fair enough; she did. So did I. During her first week, as she sobered up and her detox meds kicked in, she remained the same. She was always fussing in the kitchen, sorting out the fridge and pantry. That was my therapeutic job for the week, along with doing a stock check before giving the chef an order of what we needed. The delivery arrived. She started unpacking the food into the pantry and placed a whole load of chocolate biscuits and bars on one of the top shelves out of sight. I asked her why she'd done it. She replied, 'I know how it works in here. You're a bunch of greedy gannets.'

I was offended and furious later that day when I saw her put two bags of fun-sized Milky Ways in her large handbag. Nobody carried a handbag around in the rehab. Talk about us being greedy gannets; there she was depleting our stock, which I'd never seen done before. Two other clients told me they'd seen her put packets of biscuits in her bag.

It was Thursday, and we were due to have community group after lunch. I spoke with the therapist who was going to be running the group and told her about the situation at hand. She asked me if I'd like to be in charge of the clipboard and ask for volunteers for the therapeutic duties. Nobody likes the job of washing up, especially after dinner. It required washing the dishes the food was in, and this ate into people's phone time. I did the assigning slightly differently. I started with the washing up. I asked if anyone who hadn't been on washing up yet could please raise his or her hand. It all went well.

The therapist asked if there were any concerns, so I took a deep breath and said, 'Someone is taking chocolate biscuits and bags of fun-sized chocolates to the room. This person knows who they are.' I didn't look at anyone. I simply stared at the floor.

The therapist asked if I felt able to confront the person in group or after face-to-face. I opted for the latter. I took the woman aside in the garden, away from all our peers, and told her I'd seen her do it and so had two other people. She totally denied it, told me I was sick, and demanded I tell her who the other people were. When I refused, she lunged at me, saying, 'You're not as nice as people think. I see straight through you. You're nothing more than a stuck-up fucking bitch.'

I didn't retaliate. I went to join my peers. She followed and, for some reason, targeted my bestie, shouting at her and demanding she checked the bin in her room to prove her innocence.

The therapist who'd run the session called a meeting with the three of us in a small room. The 'thief' went first. She was ranting, crying, and denying it all. My bestie and I said very little other than to state the facts and express how her actions had led us to feel generally unsafe. We were encouraged to put the incident behind us. It would interfere with our recoveries if we clung onto it.

The afternoon was tense. I avoided her and bumped into the manager in the hallway. I told him what had happened and that I was feeling really over being there. As always, he had words of wisdom. 'Once you're out of here, you get to choose who you spend time with,' he told me. That made sense, so I hung onto that thought.

The following morning, I was alone with her in the kitchen making a mug of tea. I said, 'Morning' and asked her how she'd slept. She was pleasant, and no more food went missing after that.

My Mum wrote to me and enclosed a postcard of a beautiful wild beach. The small beach was walking distance from my house and a place I often went to sit and 'be still'. Her letter was sympathetic but explained that she and the family couldn't help me, as they all had their own issues. I felt remorse and really sad but knew I'd brought this on myself. I showed the letter to my therapist, who said, 'It shows her love and honesty.' I agreed, knowing healing would happen in God's time, not mine.

I spent a long time on my step three and presented it to the group and a therapist. I knew that I had to stay connected daily to God and practice this step throughout the day. I know that when I try and make my will conform with God's, I am safe and protected, and my path is clearer. The concept of accepting a higher power is often a major problem for addicts. I'd heard it said in AA in Sydney that 'God' could stand for good orderly direction if you disliked the concept of God. I agree with this statement. For me, God helps and guides me to have good, orderly direction in my life. All I have to do is look back at the chaos of my practising alcoholic days to see that I ran on self-will and that it *never* worked. I always ended up drunk or hurting my loved ones more. The steps are in an order for a reason. They are part of our survival kit. I've heard it said you can't stay sober through osmosis, meaning that simply going to meetings wouldn't be enough. I would not be able to 'catch' recovery by sitting next to older sober members. I would have to work the steps, be of service, and repeatedly turn my will and life over to God.

My friend the nurse was trying to get back into the rehab centre. I was talking to the manager one morning, and he said, 'She's been here three times. She needs to go somewhere different.' I thought about this and realised it was my third admission. I now knew I wouldn't be allowed back again. I think subconsciously this helped and made me more determined.

A man in his early thirties came in for detox of various drugs and alcohol. There was something strange about him, but I couldn't work out what it was. He was quite eccentric, said some pretty off-the-wall things, and drew very dark pictures in art. He wasn't offensive or aggressive, just slightly inappropriate at times. On his second day, I was outside having a cigarette with him. We were chatting normally, and then suddenly he leapt up, told me to fuck off, and proceeded to climb over the high garden fence. He slipped and cut his ear and then acted as though nothing had happened. The following night, we were due to go to our usual AA meeting. I was outside with a few other clients so missed the action inside. He'd become manic and was throwing furniture around the sitting room. He also stuffed all the paperwork from the mantelpiece down his trousers, convinced the police were coming to get him and would taser him 'down there'. The police had been called, but the damage was minimal, and nobody was injured, so they left. A member of staff escorted him to the local train station and saw him off. It was all very sad, especially as, even in that psychotic episode, he managed to write a note to us all saying he was sorry. He wrote everyone's names on it.

My CRP was identical to my previous one. I presented it on my last day. The key ring was passed around, and people said lovely things and wished me well. I was determined to stick to it this time. I was fearful of more blackout falls, dying, and the chance I may end up with 'wet brain'. I've seen this in a few people. A young lady who had three lovely young kids used to attend most of the AA meetings I attended in Sydney. We became close and encouraged each other. I hadn't seen her for nearly a month, so I asked if anyone knew whether she was OK. A man told me she had gone on a huge binge and was now in an institution, wearing adult nappies, and unable even to recognise her own kids. I've seen people with mild wet brain. Their speech is slow, and they forget what they've said, so they repeat themselves.

CHAPTER 9

RECOVERY—HOW IT WORKS

I decided to include this chapter in order to prevent repetition throughout the book. It's only possible because of all I've learnt—through AA and doing the steps and going to meetings, from others, including therapists, from books I've read, and from my own lived experiences. Remorse, resentment, and shame are feelings that have taken me back to drinking time and time again. The trail of heartache and devastation was too hard to face, the pain all-consuming, the guilt and shame crippling, so I chose to anaesthetise myself with alcohol and drugs. I believe addiction is a threefold disease—physical, emotional, and spiritual.

Alcohol kills more people than all the other drugs combined. It's legal and can be bought *everywhere.* It is seen as socially acceptable and present in celebrations and difficult situations alike. I know a lot of people who, after a hard day's work, relax with a few drinks. I also believe that if alcohol was 'discovered' today it may well be made illegal, knowing what people know now.

Defects grow in the dark and die in the exposure to light and truth. This is why honesty is such a freeing and necessary part of recovery. We all have desires and dreams which, when 'pure' and not self-seeking, will carry us to the right decisions. Desiring the will of our higher power, I believe, is key. My best thinking and desires ended up causing such an extreme sense of worthlessness, I continued drinking to blackout, knowing full well I could die.

Addiction is the disease of 'more'. I know this is true for me. I always wanted more—to be loved more, to be appreciated more, and in the end to consume more and more alcohol. The old AA saying, 'One drink is too many and a hundred not enough' was true for me. There was simply no off switch for me.

Having lived in Australia for all those years, I've been shocked by the state of the National Health Service (NHS), especially the amount of money spent on hospitalising, detoxing, and then sending back addicts to the same environment they came from. I've listened to so many addicts in the drug and alcohol centre I attend who tell me the waiting lists for rehabs are between three and six months, if not longer. Many of them are still drinking and/or using, waiting for their day to come. Some die before they get the help they desperately need. I understand how stretched financially the NHS is. But surely, in the long term, investing in more rehab facilities would be beneficial, and hospital beds would be freed up for others.

Years ago in AA, I heard the analogy of recovery as an elevator. We have the choice to decide when to get off or to carry on going down, hitting new and terrifying rock bottoms. That has certainly been my case. Even after my failed suicide attempt, I couldn't wait to get home and drink. Then there are the numerous near-death experiences I encountered, none of which stopped me from drinking. Let's not forget the *insanity* I've lived in—deluded and lying to cover up other lies and causing loved ones despair, fear, and tremendous hurt.

If you are contemplating a relapse, think very carefully. Remember how bad your last one was and be honest with yourself—no matter how badly you may be feeling, a relapse is *never* the answer. Connecting with your higher power is. As addicts, we can find ourselves in a riot of running on 'self-will', running a life revolved around ourselves. We don't care who we hurt, as long as we get our drink, hit, or fix. Self-seeking, self-centredness, and self-pity describe addicts, myself included. It's *all about me* when I'm in addiction (and it can also be that way while I'm sober) if I'm not focussed on my recovery.

Accepting and loving ourselves is how we enable growth and change. Loving myself—can't say that yet. But I can say I like who I'm becoming. Time is a precious gift; it can't be purchased or taken back. And only time will allow us to grow or allow broken relationships to heal and the trust of loved ones to be restored. Love heals. It strengthens, making us courageous both when we receive it and when we give it. In my early days in AA, I barely heard a word. But one of the only things I heard was 'how it works', which for me sums it up, with *honesty* mentioned three times. The *HOW* of AA stands for *honesty, open-mindedness*, and *willingness*. I believe honesty is the spiritual foundation of recovery. As my first sponsor said to me once, 'Why lie when the truth will do?'

The chapter 'How It Works' can be found in AA's *Big Book*, fourth edition, pages 58–60. The introduction reads:

> Rarely have we seen a person fail who has thoroughly followed our path. Those who do not recover are people who cannot or will not completely give themselves to this simple program, usually men and women who are constitutionally incapable of being honest with themselves. There are such unfortunates. They are not at fault; they seem to have been born that way. They are naturally incapable of grasping and developing a manner of living which demands rigorous honesty. Their chances are less than average. There are those, too, who suffer from grave emotional and mental disorders, but many of them do recover if they have the capacity to be honest.
>
> Our stories disclose in a general way what we used to be like, what happened, and what we are like now. If you have decided you want what we have and are willing to go to any length to get it—then you are ready to take certain steps.
>
> At some of these we baulked. We thought we could find an easier, softer way. But we could not. With all the earnestness at our command, we beg of you to be fearless and thorough from the very start. Some of us have tried to hold on to our old ideas and the result was nil until we let go absolutely.
>
> Remember that we deal with alcohol—cunning, baffling, powerful! Without help it is too much for us. But there is one who has all power—that One is God. May you find him now!
>
> Half measures availed us nothing. We stood at the turning point. We asked His protection and care with complete abandon.

Here are the steps we took, which are suggested as a program of recovery:

- Step 1. *We admitted we were powerless over alcohol—that our lives had become unmanageable.*

This is the only step that has to be done properly—100 per cent. If you haven't genuinely 'got' step one, I hate to be blunt, but you are screwed. I have been on many occasions and have to remember every day that I am most definitely powerless over alcohol.

I didn't find it hard to finally admit I was powerless over alcohol, but an older sober member in Sydney took me aside and said, 'There's a difference between admitting and accepting.' He was right. Even a monkey, if a monkey could speak, could say, 'I admit!' I had to accept with my whole being that I was, without any doubt, powerless over alcohol, and I knew my life was totally unmanageable.

This step also means accepting that we are powerless over people, places, and things. This was a whole new concept for me, as I thought I'd managed to get through life OK. The reality is my perfectionism and need to control had added to my downfall. My recovery would be at risk if I continued to think I could control these things. The only person I can control is *me*.

I can't tell you how many hours I've wasted obsessing about people, places, and things. I would have unrelenting conversations in my head, imagining what people would say, what I would say back, and so on and so on. Most of those conversations never happened. Some did, and during them, I was hell bent on being *right*.

Now, let's focus in on the second part, *unmanageable*. As my alcoholism progressed, *unmanageable* was not a strong enough word to describe my life. It wasn't a case of drinking three Bloody Marys and burning the toast or being unable to answer the phone because I was drunk; it was far more serious and dangerous. During the last nine months of my drinking, the only thing I found 'manageable' was getting hold of booze and drinking to blackout.

The *Big Book* tells us that our idea that we might become able to drink like other people has to be smashed. This is so true. My days of sipping Champagne or white wine in a ladylike manner are long gone.

It's also important to know that AA is not a religious programme. It's a spiritual one. Spirituality is the foundation of all the fellowships.

- Step 2. *Came to believe that a Power greater than ourselves could restore us to sanity.*

I found the idea that I was insane offensive, but over time, as my disease progressed, I was absolutely insane. I had no problem with the word *God* and know he is restoring my to sanity—how else could I be writing this and living free from fear? I know the God concept is a massive turn off for many people who walk through the doors of twelve-step fellowships. All I know is that it's essential to believe in something greater than you—nature, the universe, the fellowship, or whatever else works—and have the knowledge that we are *not it*. If willpower, being a great person, or doing good deeds kept us clean and sober, then the fellowship rooms would be empty.

The opposite of fear is faith. Why would we want to live in fear anymore? It is said those who have faith hit bottom harder. That has been true for me. Indescribable shame caused me to turn my back on God, as if he couldn't see what I was doing, which is ridiculous; he knows my every thought, feeling, and behaviour. He has never turned his back on me.

- Step 3. *Made a decision to turn our will and our lives over to the care of God* as we understood Him.

This step is only asking us to make a decision, a very important decision. I have had to do this with gritted teeth at times when I've hung onto anger, desired revenge, and struggled in every area of my life. Now I practice this step every day. My best thinking and willpower nearly killed me and caused horrific fear and resentment within my family.

Having hopefully found a new faith, we need to own it. We have been 'set free' from active addiction, and if we practice this step, our words, thoughts, and actions will change and keep us on the right path. We will have good and bad days. I try and see the bad days as just that and try to figure out what I've learnt from them. The *Big Book* says our higher power won't give us more than we can handle on just one day. In the past I've been furious with God and screamed at him, 'Why me?' God doesn't give us bad days; they just happen, the same way they happen to non-addicts.

- Step 4. *Made a searching and fearless moral inventory of ourselves.*

Oh shit, really?

I was told in Sydney this was the step that 'separates the boys from the men'. Though the formation of the phrase is rather sexist (remember, The *Big Book* itself was written in the 1930s), the sentiment is apt.

My first step four was shoddy. I left out things I was too ashamed to address myself, let alone share with my sponsor. My second attempt was more honest, but I hadn't grasped the main concept of 'owning your part', which meant divulging my character defects. I blamed others. My sponsor spent hours explaining how this step was supposed to be done.

It was as though I'd forgotten all I'd learnt in Sydney when I did step four in rehab. My brain was/has been pretty scrambled as a result of my drinking.

As anyone who has read my story thus far has likely gathered, my sobriety time was no 'honeymoon'. Rather, it was one drama after another, and I needed to free myself from resentments in order to stay sober. Remorse, guilt, shame, resentments, anger, fear, dishonesty, false pride, and self-loathing can make our pain so great we can relapse over any of these.

- Step 5. *Admitted to God, to ourselves, and to another human being the exact nature of our wrongs.*

Admitting to myself was hard enough. Admitting to God I found easy, as he knows everything I've thought, said, and done. But admitting my wrongs to another human being was hard.

I'd like to point out this step doesn't have to be done with a sponsor. You can choose a counsellor, preferably one who specialises in addiction, a church minister, or any ecclesiastical leader of an organised religion you belong to. I did mine with a lovely woman who is in training to be an assistant minister at the church I attend. She *knows* me. I trust and respect her.

Completing this step fully will make the progression to steps six and seven easier. This step is not about beating yourself up about what you've done. I found it to be a 'freeing' experience and a relief. As I worked through step four, my character defects became evident. I saw that, in every area, I had 'used' my defects to manipulate, coerce, blame, shame, and hurt those I love. I needed to know these things, and I have to continue daily to remind myself of the dangers of these barriers to my sobriety and happiness.

Anger is a natural feeling, often justifiable. It's also a warning sign and can lead to resentments and possible relapse. I was advised to press the pause button when angry, work out why I was feeling the anger, consider seriously how important the matter at hand is, and hand it over to God in order to prevent it festering and putting my recovery and sanity at risk.

- Step 6. *Were entirely ready to have God remove all these defects of character.*

Entirely is the key word here. Quite honestly, I love this step. My defects of character have taken me to places I never imagined I'd go. Let's be realistic. We are human beings, so naturally, our character defects will come into play again. Recognising them is the first step and giving them no power the next. I can and always will revert to some of my character defects, but stopping them in their tracks and telling them to bugger off is a must for me. Negative thinking empowers our problems, and positive energy heals and transforms us.

- Step 7. *Humbly asked Him to remove our shortcomings.*

Humility is another vital part of recovery. During my drinking career, I have had extreme false pride. Most of the time, I was feeling 'less than', but on many occasions, I felt 'better than'. Ego deflation was essential, and I needed to feel 'right-sized' humility. We humbly ask the God of our own understanding to step in and remove these unhealthy feelings, thoughts, and actions.

- Step 8. *Made a list of all persons we had harmed, and became willing to make amends to them all.*

Terrifying yes, but this step simply involves making a list and becoming willing to make amends. It doesn't say that you must rush out, saying sorry over and over again. I was guilty of doing this when I first got sober. *Sorry* doesn't cut it, not after the years and sometimes decades of harming people through our drinking and/or using.

I was terrified when I reached this step for the first time. My sponsor's wisdom helped. She turned to me and said, 'Let's deal with the fridge and get to the freezer later,' meaning *keep it simple*. I wrote a list of family members and friends and agreed I was willing to make amends to those people.

I think the question of how far you should go is a rather grey area. What if a person you've wronged is dead? What if you wronged a complete stranger who you would never see again? What about something you did while completely blacked out so honestly can't remember?

I've heard of breaking the amends down into three categories—first, *now*; second, *maybe*; and third, *never*. It works on the same principle as the fridge/freezer analogy.

The now list for me would include my kids, most of my close family, my first husband, my friends, and people whom I feel safe to do so. You may be amazed how doing this results in a shift of 'maybe' becoming a 'now' and over time, through working a solid recovery program, 'never' may also become a 'now'.

- Step 9. *Made direct amends to such people wherever possible, except when to so would injure them or others.*

This step doesn't come with any 'expiry date' or fixed time frame. It can take months or even years before you are ready to make direct amends. This step needs to be well thought out and planned carefully with your sponsor. It's crucial that the previous eight steps are firmly in place and that you are emotionally strong enough for whatever the outcome may be.

Let's look at the phrase 'injure them or others'. In some cases, making certain amends could cause further upset, shame, and hurt. You may be surprised at people's reactions when you make your amends. Some people barely remember or say, 'You weren't that bad' or 'I'd forgotten about that years ago.' Many told me they had already forgiven me, as they had later realised I was extremely sick and acted out of character.

Then there are the people who are still consumed with resentments towards you. Their reactions could prove very unsettling. But in doing this step, you are simply making your amends, with no expectations as to how they will be received. That's really important. We have worked on ourselves, identified our character defects, owned our part in all our resentments, and are now making our amends. The people we have harmed over the years may not have sought help (therapy) and could, therefore, be 'stuck' in the memories of our damaging behaviour.

I've heard it said so many times that, while we were not responsible for our actions while drinking or using, we are responsible now that we are sober. This is a comforting thought for us but a hard concept for others to get their heads around, given what we've put them through.

I mentioned planning your amends. This is crucial. You might start with a postcard, letter, or email. I wouldn't advise arranging to meet for a coffee to kick this off; suggesting it would be a good start. If the person isn't ready, leave him or her alone; you've done all you can do at that point.

A therapist during my second admission to rehab last year said something I thought was brilliant: 'Step nine is a "one-off deal".' By this, she meant it's important to help the person to whom you are making amends realise, in a polite way, that it is a 'one-off deal'—that, after you've made your amends, you would appreciate him or her not raking up the same old stuff time and time again. This is something that happens often. The people you're making amends to are so hurt and full of resentment they barely hear your apology and hang onto the past. That is their problem, not yours. You've done what you needed to do. As they say in AA, 'Your side of the street is clean.'

- Step 10. *Continued to take personal inventory and when we were wrong promptly admitted it.*

Step ten makes me think of the saying, 'Never go to bed on an argument.' Contempt breeds contempt, and small resentments can end up monumental. If you are clean and sober, you are responsible for your words and actions. Nobody is perfect, so naturally, there will be many times we think, say, and do hurtful things. But recognising yourself doing these things and apologising right there and then is important for your recovery and the people involved.

I am not up to this step yet, but I believe it can be practised every day. When I get into bed and think about my day, if I know I've upset someone, I make sure I apologise the next day.

Again, this is all about keeping our side of the street clean. Recovery demands honesty—no more lies, secrets, or acts of revenge. It's not about 'looking like the model recovering addict'; what matters is how you feel inside. I've felt so disgusted with myself over the years, but I can't change the past. I can, however, make changes for myself and my future.

- Step 11. *Sought through prayer and meditation to improve our conscious contact with God* as we understood Him, *praying only for knowledge of His will for us and the power to carry that out.*

I was physically, mentally, emotionally, and spiritually *bankrupt* when I fell through the front door of rehab for the third time. I had nothing left inside me, no fight, no hope, just desperation. The 8 a.m. mediation, which I had previously enjoyed, felt like a chore. I couldn't relax, let alone meditate while beautiful music was playing. My faith had been so real and strong at times in my life, but at this time, it was weak, and I blamed God for allowing this to happen to me again. God was not responsible.

I believe this step is all about seeking and asking for guidance, strength, and courage to live a new life, which God has planned. The more days sober I am, the easier it has become to pray. My prayer time is the most important part of my day. I know that, if I rush it or don't pray for God's will, my day can be a muddle, and I will continue running on self-will, which feels stressful. If I continue to do this, my old thinking and feelings will return, possibly leading me to relapse.

I also 'shoot arrow prayers' up throughout the day. By this, I mean pressing the pause button and saying a quick 'help me' prayer. When I put my head on my pillow at night, firstly I stretch out and think how nice it is to be alone—no offence intended to any men reading this.

I thank God every night that I'm warm, safe, clean, and sober for another day. Meditation became easier after the first few weeks in rehab. I loved listening to relaxing music, or the sound of the sea and birds. An attitude of gratitude comes in here. While drinking, I never listened to birds, watched the powerful waves of the ocean, or appreciated flowers coming into bloom; it was all about me and the bottle.

The Serenity Prayer covers it all for me. Acceptance means knowing you have to change and be guided by your higher power to know how best you can think, feel, and act during the day. I read a book recently called *God Is for the Alcoholic* (I included all addicts as I read this). I believe it's true. When I think about Jesus, I recall that he 'bothered' with people like us. He spent time with the outcasts, the 'unclean', the prostitutes and healed many by powerfully saying, 'Your sins are forgiven.'

Meditation has been clinically proven to reduce anxiety and stress and lower your blood pressure. So why wouldn't we do it? Many reasons keep us from practising meditation, among them, 'I'm too busy', 'I don't like the speaker's voice/choice of music', or simply 'I can't be bothered'. That's been me.

Meditation isn't something you can master overnight. 'Sitting with yourself' takes time and practise.

- Step 12. *Having had a spiritual awakening as the result of these steps, we tried to carry this message to alcoholics, and to practice these principles in all our affairs.*

This may be controversial, but I believe a spiritual awakening can happen before you reach this step. The fact that I'm alive, clean, and sober; that life is manageable; and that I'm doing no more harm to others is a miracle. I am guilty of the second part to a degree. I attend meetings and, as I said earlier, often feel irritated by the things people share. This is certainly not God's will; it's my ego and judgement of others.

I'm getting better at it and do try to carry the message wherever possible, especially with newcomers, people struggling, and those in the drug and alcohol centre I attend. I said earlier I've resented or skipped meetings due to laziness or torrential rain; the weather is no excuse. I remember when we were snowed in while in America. I waded through snowdrifts with my backpack in order to buy my vodka. Weather never stopped me from drinking, so why should it stop me from going to meetings?

The most important people in the rooms where AA, NA, CA, and other 'anonymous' meetings are held are the newcomers. I know how kind, supportive, and caring people were to me in Sydney meetings. We need to spread the message, take time to chat, and listen to newcomers. We need to encourage them to keep coming back and share things about ourselves so they realise we have also done awful things while drunk or high.

'How It Works' follows on with this:

Many of us exclaimed, 'What an order! I can't go through with it.' Do not be discouraged. No one among us has been able to maintain anything like perfect adherence to these principles. We are not saints. The point is that we are willing to grow along spiritual lines. The principles we have set down are guides to progress. We claim spiritual progress rather than spiritual perfection.

Our description of the alcoholic, the chapter to the agnostics, and our personal adventures before and after make clear three pertinent ideas

- a) That we were alcoholic and could not manage our own lives.
- a) That probably no human power could have relieved our alcoholism.
- b) That God could and would if He were sought.

I'll stop there, as it's all in the *Big Book*. Please don't think you can do the steps on your own. I've heard people say they've done them with God or on their own. As I mentioned earlier, I tried this myself during my first recovery, which led to months of insanity and fear. There are totally valid reasons we need a sponsor. With the exception of step five, which can be done with a religious leader of the faith you practice, going through the steps *with a sponsor* is a must.

When I first talked about the twelve steps with Mum during my first recovery, she became extremely interested and said to me many times, 'These are steps for a better life not just for addicts but for people in general. If non-addicted people adhered to them, their lives and those of their loved ones would be far more harmonious, and their destructive thinking and behaviours would lessen considerably'.

Choosing a sponsor can be tricky. In early recovery, our minds are all over the place. I know I went with the first woman who sounded good when she shared at a meeting. Changing sponsors is fine. We grow out of some. Things change in our lives and theirs. I've done it a few times and never felt judged or rejected by my sponsor. 'Doing' the steps is great, but it's a lifelong process. Steps need to be revisited. Or, as was true in my case, you may need to go back to step one and do them all again.

As I mentioned in the introduction, there was so much I wanted to say. And during periods of sobriety, I often thought about the psychiatrist I was under the care of in Sydney, and her suggestion of me writing a book. The combination of these things led me to think, *Maybe, just maybe, I could write a book.* The idea was ludicrous, given I was in early recovery, but I believe God prompted me and has guided and protected me as I've divulged the absolute truth of where addiction has taken me. I am officially the Rehab/Therapy Queen. But I know, without any doubt, that knowledge won't keep me sober. I've known a lot of highly intelligent and/or arrogant people in AA. These are two qualities that will definitely not keep you sober. Humility, honesty, open-mindedness, and willingness to go to any lengths will. Intelligence and knowledge are admirable qualities, but no one can think or rationalise him or herself sober.

The AA slogans provide simple reminders of the path to stay on. I've chosen to include some rather than all. I recommend looking them up on the internet.

- *Easy does it*—I need to remind myself of this. No more manic gardening, as the only reason I act like this is because I can't sit with myself.
- *First things first*—Recovery must come first. I need to pace myself and do what needs to be done for my recovery, sanity, and general well-being. I'm a huge list writer. I love the feeling of ticking off things I've done. But I need to prioritise what's important for each day and not feel like I've failed if I haven't ticked everything off my list—there's always tomorrow!
- *Live and let live*—Yes, *live*. We are alive, thank God. Recovery doesn't have to be boring. New opportunities will come our way, especially if we are ready take a risk and go for it. What's the worst

thing that can happen? You don't enjoy the new opportunity or fail at it? That's fine. As for *let live*, I believe this means simply letting others live their lives and make their own mistakes. Don't judge. Instead, come alongside them and encourage them.

- *But for the grace of God*—This is my favourite slogan. By the grace of God, I'm free from the *hell* of active addiction. Healing has begun with certain family members, and I'm free to dream of what lies ahead for me.
- *Think ... think ... think*—I despised this slogan in the early days. All I did was think. I was drowning in self-pity. I hated myself. And as I relived over and over in my mind all the chaos and devastation I'd caused, I felt as though my head would explode. Now I see it differently. This slogan reminds us to think about how we are feeling, acknowledge any sad or bad feelings, and think of a way to turn our thinking around.
- *One day at a time*—That's all we have. Enjoy and celebrate the fact you are clean and sober, becoming a functioning person, and not causing any more harm to loved ones.
- *Let go and let God*—That's it. Take your hands off the steering wheel and allow God to guide and protect you.

There are a few additional helpful reminders I'd like to share with you:

- *Act as if*—I was advised, 'Fake it until you make it in the early days.' It seemed rather wrong, as I'd lived a life of 'eyes and teeth'. But it does work.
- *This too shall pass*—I never felt it would, but it did.
- *I can't ... he can ... I think I'll let him*—Yes, let God do for you what you can't do for yourself.
- *If it works, don't fix it*—This advice is true. It's working for me and can work for you.
- *Keep coming back; it works if you work it*—I've had to force myself to go to meetings but know it will continue to work if I am prepared to put the work in.
- *Keep right-sized*—Oops. I've been chronically wrong-sized over the years. It's important never to forget where you came from

and your last 'drunk'. You don't do this to berate yourself, but to remind yourself of what you'd be going back to if you decided to drink or use again.

- *Sobriety is a journey, not a destination*— 'Doing' recovery isn't a walk in the park, but it sure beats living in addiction.
- *Poor me … poor me … pour me another drink*—That was me,
- *To thine own self be true*—The truth sets us free. In sobriety, standing in the truth of yourself is a must. No more lies, judging, plotting revenge, and making yourself crazy in the head. Be true to yourself. Speak up when you're feeling good and when you're struggling.
- *I came, I came to, I came to believe*—See steps one and two.
- *Live in the now*—That's all we have.
- *If God seems far away, who moved?*—Me.
- *Turn it over*—See step three.
- *AA-altered attitudes*—Our attitudes needed to change, not just towards others but also towards ourselves and life.
- *Nothing is so bad, a drink won't make it worse*—This is a hard truth. I drank to escape. But when I sobered up, the same problems were there. And in many cases, they'd been compounded due to my behaviour while drinking.
- *We are only as sick as our secrets*—I touched on this earlier, and I believe it's true.
- *I can't handle it, God. You take over*—This is another way of saying, 'Let God take the steering wheel.'
- *Keep an open mind*—My mind was closed for years, especially to AA. I saw it as a life sentence of misery, which is not the case. Being open-minded is a gift that allows us to remain teachable and learn through others and through our own life experiences.
- *Willingness is the key*—Willingness is the key to freedom. I often pray for the willingness to be willing, if that makes sense.
- *More will be revealed*—As recovery progresses, so do we. Our thoughts, feelings, and outlook on life change. We begin to experience self-worth and self-esteem and even to like the person we've become.
- *You will be amazed*—Yes, I am amazed, again. I am amazed I'm actually writing this, given I'm in very early recovery.

- *No pain, no gain*—One of the AA promises reads, 'We shall not regret the past nor wish to shut the door on it.' Nothing is wasted. All the pain is in the past, and if we hadn't gone through it, recovery wouldn't feel so amazing.
- *Do it sober*—Doing anything sober is far more fun.
- *Sober and crazy*—Yes, I've been both. In fact, I've been more crazy sober than when I was drunk; after all, I was drinking to blackout, so had no feelings or thoughts.
- *Pass it on*—You can only keep what you have by passing it on.
- *Either you is or you ain't*—You can't be half pregnant. You are either an addict or not on addict. There's no in between.
- *Before you say, 'I can't', say, 'I'll try'.*
- *Practice an attitude of gratitude*—I do. I'm grateful every day that I'm no longer a slave to alcohol and drugs and I'm not causing any more harm to my loved ones.
- *Don't pick up a drink, pick up the phone instead*—This was a saying I initially *hated*. When I returned from relapses, I was asked by a quite a few people in AA, 'Why didn't you pick up the phone rather than a drink?' *Bloody marvellous question*, I would think. And my answer was always the same: 'I'm an alcoholic.' Each time, the relapse had been creeping up on me for weeks, and I drank. In the early days, it used to baffle me when people said, 'I found myself in the bottle shop.' *How ridiculous!* I would think. But this was to become my story time and time again. I believe a relapse starts in your brain weeks, even months before you actually drink. I was asked to do a 'relapse egg' at the rehab in Sydney. When I presented it to the therapist and group, it was extremely easy to see—I had allowed resentments to fester and/or develop into uncontrollable anger. Feeling hard done by, plotting revenge—all of these would take up my entire thought process until it became unbearable, so I would drink. Sadly, as many of us know, when we sober up, the bad thoughts are still there. So we continue drinking to escape.

We all have choices. For example, we can decide if today is going to be a good or bad day. And yes, of course, there will be bad days. But none will be as bad our worst day in active addiction. We've regretted the past, dreaded the future, and been less than thrilled about the present. I have experienced all of these feeling and thoughts. But now I don't regret the past. It's in the past, so let it stay there. I don't dread the future, as I know if I continue to do whatever it takes to maintain my sobriety, I need never drink again. As for now, I'm hopeful. I have dreams, which feels pretty strange and almost unbelievable given my past.

Routine is very important in recovery. It's something we lose in addiction. I know I had no routine other than drinking.

Forcing ourselves to do the opposite of what our mind is telling us—that's been a hard one for me. Again, that's me running on self-will, which can be a block to my recovery.

I know the importance of taking one day at a time. But I believe setting goals and daring to dream are really important. They spur us on and give us hope and a sense that life will be an adventure, rather than boring. I have learnt that I can take care of myself, and I have learnt that what I can't do, God will do for me.

Depression is very common in recovery, but it feeds itself. I believe looking after ourselves physically, mentally, and spiritually will be the solution to our depression. Recovery is not a 'do-it-yourself' programme. We need the fellowship, a sponsor, and the willingness to turn our will and lives over to the God of our own understanding. In addiction, life had little or no meaning. Through working the steps, we become part of life. In recovery, it's important to stop—to pause and take a look at your progress.

I believe the most important relationships are my relationship with God, and then the relationship I have with myself. The latter is a 'work in progress'

Even though I am a great believer in AA, there are other programmes available. There are alcohol therapy clinics; SMART recovery (Self Management and Recovery Training), a non-profit that provides assistance to those seeking abstinence from addictive behaviours; and other programmes.

I'd like to finish by saying that I've 'done' recovery obsessively through fear, or to the best of my ability at times, and I've also done it half-heartedly or not at all. Bearing this in mind, it's imperative I don't forget how each of these felt. I also need to remind myself that it's 'progress, not perfection' I'm aiming for.

CHAPTER 10

THIS HAS TO BE IT

I left rehab on 12 December. When I walked through my front door, not only did I feel very different, but so did my house. The 'crime scene', as I had often referred to it, no longer felt like a crime scene. It felt safe as I wandered from room to room, remembering the places I had woken up—on floors, halfway down the stairs, and even on the paved patio. I had experienced a lot living in a rehab with, at times, twelve other clients, and I had learnt so much about myself through being there and with the help of the therapists and all the other members of the centre's staff. I knew that all the relapses, rehabs, therapy, and life in general had taught me a great deal about myself. I can't say I skipped out of the front door happy, joyous, and free. However, I knew I stood a very good chance of remaining clean and sober if I continued to believe that the God of my understanding was a loving, forgiving God who, if I stayed in daily contact and turned my life and will over to him daily, would continue to do for me that which I could not do for myself.

I had a detailed yet realistic plan for my first week at home. It included getting up at the same time each day, prayer and meditation, daily readings, followed by breakfast, and then planning where I needed to be and at what time during the day. I also made sure I ate lunch and dinner and allowed myself time to unwind before a set bedtime. This may sound rather rigid, but I knew I needed this healthy, balanced routine. I'd been full of good intentions when I returned home after my first two admissions, but my emotional sobriety was on very shaky ground, and it didn't take long before

I slipped into bad habits, which ultimately led me back to drinking. I saw this new regime, not so much as a chore but more like a map for a much better life.

One of my favourite daily readings is a book called *The Language of Letting Go*, by Melody Beattie. Here are a few powerful statements I've recently read. First, 'God help me know I am being guided into what's good about life, especially when I feel confused and without direction. Help me trust enough to wait until my mind and vision are clearer and consistent. Help me find clarity.' Second, 'God, help me let go of fear, doubt, and confusion—the enemies of self-trust. Help me go forward in peace and confidence. Help me grow in trust for myself and you, one day at a time, one experience at a time.'

My day begins with a mug of tea and a cigarette. I often think how lovely that first mug of tea tastes, as well as the other drinks throughout the day. I drank alcohol for the effect, not the taste, from the moment I switched from wine to vodka in America. After my morning prayer time and daily readings, I lie on the couch listening to one of the worship CDs my sister gave me when I first moved back. I also listen to meditation apps of soft music or sounds of nature, which one of the rehab staff members kindly downloaded for me. It's taken me until now to focus, and my mind still wanders off at times. I find breathing techniques work really well. Sometimes I lie on the couch and breath slowly, hand on my stomach as I feel the rise and fall. If I find it too hard to concentrate, I count in and out breaths, which frees up my mind. I practice mindfulness while out, walking to the bus, or on walks. To me, mindfulness is quite simply an appreciation of the present. Being *present* is one of the best presents of all in recovery. Staying safe is a priority for me; I only see certain people and avoid anyone who I know could trigger me.

My last 'drunk' hadn't been as bad as the previous ones, as there were only a few unexplained bruises. But I knew I was mentally, emotionally, and spiritually *dead*. I had reached an all-time low. I realise now I needed this in order to be forced to my knees and to surrender *totally*.

My new sponsor, who as I've mentioned is tough but loving, had only a few expectations of me. Firstly, I needed to go to an AA meeting every day for ninety days. Secondly, I was to phone her every day. And lastly, I needed to begin working the steps straight away. I did steps one, two, and three in two weeks. We discussed them over coffees. She needed to know they were firmly in place before I moved onto step four.

The 'ninety meetings' requirement filled me with dread. I have to be honest and say I didn't go to nearly as many as she'd suggested. I missed my meetings in Sydney, where there was amazing experience, strength, and hope. The meetings in my area are so different; there are a few that I love going to, but the rest often leave me feeling resentful and with a sense of impending doom. Please don't think I'm judging the members.

I have a log burner in my sitting room that hadn't been used the previous winter. I decided putting it to use would be not just economical but also lovely. I envisioned lying on the couch in the evenings watching the flames. I ordered wood from a local man. When he arrived, he asked me to move my car so that he could put it in the garage. I froze for a moment and then began digging myself into a ridiculous hole. I told him my mum had the keys; she was borrowing it for a few days. 'Don't you have a second set?' he asked. I told him my neighbour had them in case they ever needed to move my car when I was away. I don't know why I didn't just come out and tell him the truth.

My neighbour tried starting my car, which hadn't been driven in over a year. The battery was flat, and the men with the wood were due back any minute. I asked them to just put the wood in the driveway. They did, and two of my neighbour's young sons stacked it in the garage for me.

I went to the local cemetery to gather kindling for my burner. I was snapping and snipping the dead wood when I stopped and looked around. It wasn't the gravestones that caught my eye. It was the fact that here I was, clean and sober, gathering kindling. I sat and had a cigarette, thinking how very different my life was. It's the simple things that make me happy. I had walked through that cemetery hundreds of times to and from the bus stop, but now I could see the beauty. One of the things I love about this country is the seasons—so different from Australia. I started actually looking at the trees and budding plants as I walked. I've seen the trees bare in the winter and then buds appearing and, finally, lush green trees, beautiful daffodils, snowdrops, and wild garlic and flowers. My bus trips had become enjoyable as I sat looking out at the sea, the spring plants, and the flowers emerging.

I had finally *stopped* racing from one thing to another, anxious, regretting the past, fearful of the future, having unrealistic expectations of myself and others, and imagining what sort of disastrous things may happen. I realised I was no longer a prisoner in my own head and house. Reflecting on how I drank made me feel exhausted. Those days were filled with constant scheming, adrenaline-fuelled walks up to the local shops with my backpack, and prayers that no would see me buying the bottles. I live in a small village and was told months later when I was sober that I had, indeed, been seen. Let's not forget the text messages. I dreaded messages, especially from my kids. It would take me half an hour to type a short note saying how busy I was and that I'd catch up soon. I would lie on the couch, drunk, temporarily safe. A car door slamming made me jump, and a knock on the door was the final straw. I needed to drink faster, pass out, and be oblivious to the world. I had led such a lonely existence. But that's how I'd chosen to live when I was drinking.

I thought I'd put that previous paragraph in to remind me what my drinking life was like. It's such a huge contrast to my life now. I'm living in the moment, taking each day one at a time. This is a safe and beautiful thing. When I first got sober in Sydney, I used to think, *How can I possibly fill my days without alcohol?* All I knew was 'drink, try to function and not get found out, drink, sleep, drink, lie, isolate'. And the thought of all those hours in the day without alcohol was terrifying. I remember ringing my sponsor in Sydney when I was ten months sober and saying I felt bored. She replied, 'Maybe you have serenity.' I thought about this and had to agree. I wasn't bored. I was functioning, calm, and feeling good.

In this recovery, I can't say I wake up, leap out of bed, throw my arms in the air, and feel incredible. I wake up around four-thirty or five o'clock every morning. I've no idea why but accept it and proceed to do everything I need to do to maintain and improve my recovery. After my first mug of tea and cigarette, I stand in the garden and look at the moon and stars in awe. I couldn't have cared less about them when I was drinking.

Eating properly has always been an issue for me in early recovery. But I know it's important to avoid any of the HALTS (hungry, angry, lonely, tired, stressed). Our bodies actually crave sugar once we are off the booze, which is full of it. My weight gain is not a product of healthy eating. Living alone, I get bored and lazy at the thought of meals. I fill my fridge with healthy food. I'm always full of good intentions, rather like I was with my drinking, and hope the day will be different and I will put healthy food in me. By the evening, if I am tired, I often struggle to eat a proper meal, so I resort to a large piece of cheesecake or a few Bounty bars. As an addict, I can't do 'just one' when it comes to most things. It's two chocolate bars, four biscuits, and so on. I keep promising myself I won't buy these things, but every time I go shopping, they seem to end up in my trolley!

My now-present 'muffin top' won't kill me. Alcohol will, which is why I'm not beating myself up about it. I'm just grateful it's winter and thankful for leggings and long, baggy tops! This time a year ago, I was a stone and a half lighter, I was incredibly frail, and could barely walk. I was literally drinking myself to death. So as I said, the muffin top is not a problem!

I still drink alcoholically, not alcohol but tea, squash, and ginger beer. I counted the other morning how many mugs of tea I'd had between 5 and 8 a.m. (that's when I'm writing *Dying for a Drink*). It was seven, plus a cigarette with each one. I never drink out of a wine glass. That's my personal choice. I don't drink non-alcoholic wine or Champagne either. For me, that's association, and I'm not prepared to take the risk that one day, I'll put real wine in a glass and will then be 'off again'. I've heard of people doing this, progressing to low-alcohol beer, and then finding themselves back to drinking the way they had before.

Returning to my activities at the drug and alcohol centre was great. The allotment doesn't need much doing. We spend our time digging over vegetable plots and covering them for the winter. We sit around the fire, drink mugs of tea, and chat.

I reached out for help when I was struggling mentally; this was something I had been reluctant to do. My pride, and the hard-wired sense of 'having to look OK' prevented me doing this, which was incredibly foolish, as so many people wanted to help me.

Going back to church was the most important thing for me. I felt a sense of belonging there, and the minister who had faithfully visited me at home and texted me while I was in rehab gives me strength and hope with every sermon. I sit with my friend and another friend of my Mum's who is part of the 'Monday Girls'. I know they and many others have been praying for a long time for me to be 'set free from the obsession to drink'.

I went for the well-overdue check-up X-ray of my shoulder. The bone had healed, but there was a slight bump just below my bra strap. I was offered surgery to correct it but refused. It would be for cosmetic reasons primarily, and I knew how much *I loved anaesthetics*. I have the constitution of an ox due to my excessive drinking and drug taking and used to actually ask the anaesthetist to give me it slowly—now that's pretty sick! I remember being able to count back from ten to five; this was highly unusual, and the staff must have been surprised.

One day at a time has never felt more real. I only have today, and if I let my mind wander into the past or future, it's only a matter of time before my thinking becomes irrational and/or obsessive and I could easily pick up a drink.

Unnecessary worrying has led me to incredibly negative emotional head spaces. I'm not just talking about the past twelve years; my life in general has often been complicated and/or compromised by worrying. In the Gospel of Matthew 6:25–34, it states, 'Can any one of you by worrying add a single hour to your life?' Profound words indeed.

In the early weeks, I rang the rehab I'd been in at least once a week to let them know how I was doing. Paranoia set in, and I thought maybe I shouldn't ring them, but every staff member I spoke with said they loved hearing from me and any clients who were doing well. I often got through to the manager, which was great. His calm, witty, and insightful words were always a relief.

Simple things like *actually* writing a gratitude list each night have really helped me. I used to do this regularly. As with many things, I would be 'gung-ho'. I would start something and give up after a short time. But this is something I do every night now. Some nights, it's easy. Others, it feels repetitive, as I'm always grateful to be alive, sober, and not causing any more harm. But if I take just a bit more time, I am able to write loads, as my days now are *so* dramatically different from those in the past.

A week before Christmas, I did an online grocery shop. I got to the bit where it says 'choose your delivery spot', and every one was taken. This would have caused me massive anxiety in the past. But I caught the bus into town and got everything I needed. I have always disliked the whole pre-Christmas hype, people buying frantically in excess when the shops are only shut for one day.

One of the things in my CRP was to volunteer in one of the local charity shops. I was picking up some groceries in the village and had some heavy items so decided to catch the bus up the hill. It wasn't due for fifteen minutes, and I was standing outside one of the charity shops. I believe God gave me the courage to walk in and ask if the shop needed any volunteers. The woman who runs the shop said yes, on Wednesday mornings. So I filled in a short form and arranged to start on Wednesday, 4 January.

My kids came to stay on 21 December for Christmas. They kept saying how well I looked, and I did leave the cooking and tree decorating for their arrival as my son had suggested. They also said they didn't want or need to drink while with me, which showed their love and respect for me, as well as how much they want me well. It took away some of my fear of one or both of them becoming addicts. I believe genetics has a lot to do with this disease, so I pray that they don't end up like me. On the positive side, if they did, I would be present and able to come alongside them and be of use.

Both kids, through diversity, my addiction, and other radical curveballs thrown their way, are incredible young adults. They are kind, caring, and outward looking, and they have a deep sense of equality. Their unconditional love for me has always been there. That's not to say they've necessarily liked me or my behaviour, but they've never given up on me. Now that's 'priceless' and the most cherished part of my recovery.

During my most desperate times, I would gain comfort by thanking God for them being so well adjusted, in spite of me. The loving and supportive response from family, friends, and therapists was, 'It's because, not in spite, of you.'. I really struggled with this and still do at times. My therapist asked me to write down my loveliest memories of their childhood. There it was, in black and white—precious years during which I'd done my absolute best and loved every minute.

My best friends never drink in front of me. In fact, I don't spend time with anyone who drinks. My neighbours both invited me to Christmas and New Year's Day parties, which was kind, but they understood why I declined their offers, as alcohol would be there.

My Mum picked us up on 23 December and took us to her place. We had a lovely afternoon. The kids decorated the tree, Mum pottered around putting up lights and Christmas things, and I put the batteries in Dad's singing and dancing toys. I was finally back in my favourite seat in the kitchen; it's squashed between the wall and the end of the kitchen table. We sat there drinking a mug of tea and chatting, and I remembered all the happy times I'd sat on that chair during my visits.

The kids and I spent Christmas Eve cooking together for the next day. We lay on couches watching films, log burner roaring, and the tree (done by the kids) looking gorgeous. They knew I would be going to church at 11 a.m. on Christmas Day. My daughter had already said she would like to come with me, and to my surprise, my son said he wanted to come too. I was thrilled, and sitting in between them in church was the highlight of the day for me. The minister welcomed them by name, which spoke volumes.

My daughter left early on Boxing Day. She went to stay with her new boyfriend and his family. I was going to wake my son at 11 a.m., when there was a knock on the front door. I opened it and was speechless. There stood my nephew, whose wedding I'd missed, along with his sister and her boyfriend. They stayed for a quick coffee but both hugged me and said, 'You are still our auntie.' Those words and their presence gave me an amazing feeling, given how much I'd hurt their mum.

The healing with Mum had begun. It felt great. She had invited my son and me for lunch that day, and my brother and his family would be there. My son and I went to Mum's for lunch. I felt nervous about seeing my brother and his family, but it was a wonderful day. My son was fast-tracked with his second degree, as he already had a Bachelor of Science. He did years one and two in one year and is now in his third year. During lunch, he got into a wonderful discussion with my brother about his coursework. They share the same passion, and it was lovely to watch, as everybody else, including me, had virtually no idea what they were talking about.

My brother drove us home and played a game of chess with my son. I loved seeing them play and really appreciated my brother's support and love for me.

I knew that, when my son left, I would be at risk of slipping back into unhealthy habits—not going to AA meetings because it was freezing and wet or just feeling lonely and sad. I had to force myself to do the opposite of what my mind was telling me and to 'keep moving forward'. It's an *action* programme. And it's good to take healthy risks. If I didn't try new things, I would be stuck. And it wouldn't be long before boredom, isolation, and resentment would kick back in.

The day after my son left, my two best friends came for dinner with their kids, who are young adults. We had a lovely evening and sat chatting in the sitting room after dinner with the log burner lit. My god-daughter stayed the night, which was lovely. The following day, her mum picked us up to go and see the house our other friend and husband had bought nearby. It's a gorgeous family home with a large garden and overlooks beaches and beautiful countryside. Personally I'm thrilled, as it means they will be living near me by the end of this year.

After having my kids stay with me during Christmas and hosting friends and their kids in my house, I thought, *How wonderful. My home is starting to have new happy memories.* These new memories were so unlike the past, when my home had felt 'dark' and lonely, and all I had done was drink, isolate, and damage those I loved.

My New Year's Eve consisted of baked beans on toast for dinner; going to an evening AA meeting, which was packed; and then heading home and getting in bed by 10 p.m. As I lay in bed, I thought, *Bugger off, 2016. That was shit.* Then I prayed that 2017 would be a clean and sober year for me and that life would take on new meaning and I wouldn't cause any more chaos or hurt to my loved ones.

On New Year's Day, I rang my mum and asked if she would like a hand the following Friday to take down all the Christmas things. She was without Dad and, I knew, missing him terribly. She jumped at the idea and said, 'Shall we grab a bite to eat afterwards?'

Words can't express how I felt—gratitude, love, and a knowing that healing with Mum was really beginning. I was in town on a Monday and found a card in the Christian bookshop with the same proverb my minister had preached on a few weeks before. 'Trust in the Lord with all your heart and lean not on your own understanding. In all your ways acknowledge him and he shall make your path straight' (Proverbs 3:5–6). I sent it to Mum with a handwritten prayer from *The 12 Step Prayer Book*, entitled 'Let Go, Let God'. It reads:

- To 'let go' does not mean to stop caring; it means I can't do it for someone else.
- To 'let go' is not to enable, but to allow learning from natural consequences.

- To 'let go' is to admit powerlessness, which means the outcome is not in my hands.
- To 'let go' is not to try to change or blame another; it's to make the most of myself.
- To 'let go' is not to care for but to care about.
- To 'let go' is not to fix but to be supportive.
- To 'let go' is not to judge but to allow another to be a human being.
- To 'let go' is not to protect; it's to permit another to face reality.
- To 'let go' is not to deny but to accept.
- To 'let go' is not to nag, scold, or argue but instead to search out my own shortcomings and correct them.
- To 'let go' is not to adjust everything to my desires but to take each day as it comes and cherish myself in it.

I posted it to Mum just before my first shift in the charity shop. When I met Mum on the Friday, she thanked me for the card and prayer but thought the prayer was about me! I laughed and said, 'No, Mum. It's for you. I totally understand why you had to stand back and not see me for ten months. You needed to keep yourself safe.' We had a wonderful afternoon and early dinner in a new restaurant in the village. I got into bed feeling so happy and slept for ten hours—that hadn't happened in years.

While I acknowledge this book is about 'me' and the horrific truth about addiction, I hope and pray that people who are dealing with loved ones in addiction will find some encouragement and comfort from the 12 Step Prayer above. There is plenty of help available to provide you with support and make you aware you are not alone in your struggle. 'Al-Anon/Alateen are worldwide fellowships that offer a program of recovery for the families and friends of alcoholics, whether or not the alcoholic recognises the existence of a drinking problem or seeks help.' I know, from talking to people in your situation, how valuable and life-changing this decision to seek help for yourselves is; it will benefit not only you but also your loved ones, whom you desperately want to see get well.

I felt nervous walking into the charity shop for my first shift, but at the same time, I was thrilled to be walking in as me, not just an alcoholic. My first day was spent taking down all the Christmas things from the window display and being taught how to use the till. During my last hour, I steamed new articles of clothing ready to be put out for sale. I walked out of there feeling marvellous—now that's a feeling I hadn't experienced in years.

My Wednesdays at the charity shop became more interesting. I progressed to using the till alone, and my first mistake was to put in a hundred pounds rather than ten pounds. The staff were lovely and graciously guided me when it came to things I wasn't sure about. I was shocked to learn—and it's an eye-opener to people in general—that the shop dealt with regular shoplifters. I can't comprehend anyone doing this in a charity shop, of all places.

A lovely old man came in one day and handed me two books he was donating. He also gave a clear bag with loads of coins, including one-pound coins. The manager came out, thanked him, and told me he does this once a month.

He was a far cry from a rather posh-looking older couple, who came in and looked at a beautiful vase with a forty-pound sticker on it. She asked if I'd take thirty for it. I was new at this but managed to say, 'If you look on the bottom, you will see it's Darlington crystal, undamaged and priced to sell.' They looked at me as if I was some sort of lowlife, sighed, and said, 'We'll take it.'

We get a lot of mums in with their young kids. The families would be looking for clothes, the kids would be mucking around, and the mums would look stressed. I would offer to play with the kids in the corner where we kept kids toys and books. I love kids, and it feels so good helping others; this was a huge contrast from my drinking days, when all that mattered was me and making sure I had enough booze.

I put off my step four until after Christmas. I knew it would be far larger and more painful than the last one I had done in Sydney. So much had happened since then, and the consequences of my drinking had been far more destructive to myself and to my loved ones. I made various attempts at it and got overwhelmed time and time again. I explained what was happening to my sponsor, who said, 'It's not a race. Take all the time you need.'

I got distressed doing it one morning, and my sponsor's phone went straight to voicemail. So I rang the rehab centre. I was so relieved to speak to the manager. He listened, and as always, words of wisdom came out of his mouth. He said, 'Think about it. Maybe it's a step-three problem.' He was right. I needed to turn my will over to God to continue with this step. He also said, 'If you find it stressful again, simply put it aside and go back to it later.' I completed the step a few weeks later, and as mentioned in the previous chapter, I did step five with the lovely lady from church.

By the grace of God, I haven't ended up on the streets begging or selling my body for booze. But I know that could be me if I don't put my recovery first. And I do mean *first*—above people, including my kids, and my own complacency, which I've been prone to and still can be. That means I have to be aware that I'll make excuses not to go to meetings or the drug and alcohol centre and kid myself that I'm doing OK. I may be for the moment, but soon I'll be in serious danger. It could be a week, a month, or even a year, and I'll find myself drinking and wave goodbye to my *life* and all I've worked hard for.

I treated myself to a five-day stay at the Christian retreat. I had so many wonderful memories of Dad there. But unlike previous visits, during which I'd sobbed, felt desperately alone, and missed him terribly, I sat calmly and 'chatted away' to him. I know what he would be saying if he was still alive: 'Daught, you can do this, trust in the Lord with all your heart, and he will set you free'. The managers of the retreat were my prayer ministers. We worked through some unresolved issues, and they prayed powerfully. We have become wonderful friends, and they have continued to love and support me.

I ordered a packed lunch every day and walked to the beautiful wild beach below the retreat and up onto the Bryn, which has amazing views. During one of my walks, I sat on a rock eating my sandwiches. The sky was grey. The sun broke through a few times, and at that moment, I knew *God had set me free from the obsession to drink.*

An assistant minister in church had preached about Jesus healing the paralysed man, how his friends had carried him and lowered him through the roof in order to get to him to Jesus. It was the faith of the paralysed man's friends Jesus saw. And he said, 'Your sins are forgiven.' The man stood up and walked. This story made me think of all the people who had been praying for me. So much of the time I was incapable of praying for myself due to being drunk. I believe God acts on the faith and prayers of others, and I am so grateful for all the people who have prayed and still pray for me. I haven't thought about a drink since I went into rehab for the third time. I'd queried whether God had set me free, but now I knew.

My brother and two of his daughters drove down to Wales and stayed with Mum for a night. They'd been thinking of getting a dog for years, and now finally they were going to take the plunge. They went to look at a litter of puppies that had born on Christmas Day at a place in the centre of Wales. My brother has always wanted a male dog and joked about the lack of testosterone in their house—he has a wife and three daughters—so a male was chosen. They named him Wilson. I've seen pictures of him on Facebook. He's adorable, and I know he will be loved and cherished. While he was staying, he popped over to see me. I was speechless when I opened the door. He hadn't had to make the effort, but he did. And so more healing within my family was happening. Yay!

My friend whom I sit with in church mentioned a book that Dad had read years ago and was going to see if she could get me a copy. The next day at 'Monday Girls', my Mum was waving it around asking if anyone wanted to read it. My friend was thrilled and offered to give it to me. But Mum said she would like to give it to me herself. She rang me up and asked if I fancied a walk the following Sunday afternoon. I jumped at the opportunity—more healing and time with Mum were two things I'd longed for. She drove us down to the beach. We sat on a bench where Dad's ashes had been scattered and then did a wonderful coastal walk. It was like old times. We chatted and laughed, and I could see in her eyes how thrilled she was to see me looking so healthy and sounding hopeful and excited about the future.

My two best friends, who arranged for me to go into rehab on three occasions have and still are an amazing support. They have loved and cared for me, and I can't imagine the fear they have lived in, waiting for a phone call telling them I was dead. We had talked a lot while having our cream teas on Sundays. I was having trouble with an important concept—the fact that I'm not just an alcoholic. Both of them, and our friend who lives in Australia, have, and still do, encourage me to see myself as 'me', not just an alcoholic. I believe this is an issue many addicts suffer with, especially while in active addiction, as our entire lives revolve around booze and drugs. I am *unbelievably* blessed to have such incredible friends. Our friendship has spanned decades, and even though I lived away for all those years, we have remained best friends.

I was going out every day of the week, which was important for my recovery but meant I was exhausted by the evenings. I was watching TV one night and woke up at 2 a.m. fully dressed and dazed and with that awful old feeling. It took me at least five minutes to realise where I was and that I hadn't been drinking. I had a mug of tea and a cigarette to wake myself up. I felt intense relief that I was sober and went straight to bed.

The following morning when I was in the shower, I stopped and thought, *How amazing.* This was the same bathroom where I had come to on the floor. Here was where I had been delusional—the toilet was on the ceiling, and there was no bath! I shower every day, and I brush my teeth twice a day. That never happened when I was drinking. It comes back to the importance of routine and self-care. I now do these things without even thinking about it, I now put the right-coloured bin bags out on Wednesday nights. I used to stagger out in the dark and have to check what the neighbours had put out when I was drinking. If I was in blackout, the bins didn't go out at all. Wearing pyjamas and sleeping in my bed are another example of how I've changed. I barely slept in my bed at all while drinking since my move back to the UK. I always woke up on the floor or, if lucky, on the couch. These may sound like small things, but reflecting on these changes is a good reminder of how far I've come.

Mum told me when I was first in recovery that her prayer for me was that I 'may become the women God intended'. It was a lovely prayer, but that didn't happen. My disease progressed, and things got massively worse. I now value that prayer and know that, if I keep my eyes focussed on Jesus, I will become that women. I don't know what this will entail yet, but don't need to know as it's in God's hands not mine which is such a relief.

I admire people I see in town wearing large boards around their necks proclaiming about God and Jesus. It takes so much courage and makes me realise what a coward I am. I had to think hard about how I would bring my faith into this book, fearing it would offend some people. I understand what it's like to have no faith, to be angry with God, and to feel like a total failure who would be better off dead. As I said in the beginning, a belief in something greater than you is vital, along with the knowledge that you cannot be your own higher power—it won't work.

Hope is the key to unlocking discouragement. When we're discouraged, it's a warning sign, telling us that we've wandered over the God line. Our higher power wants us to prosper, grow, and fulfil our wildest (healthy) dreams. I believe the secret to success is in acknowledging our limitations. I mentioned earlier, I have had to stop writing *Dying for a Drink* numerous times, tears pouring down my cheeks as I relived the horrors of my past and the destruction I caused. I believe tears are good. They are healing and a great way of getting rid of our sadness. I also believe getting angry is good. I have thumped pillows and cushions and screamed at the top of my voice on beaches when there is no one around. Anger needs to be let out and then discarded. Otherwise, it will turn into all-consuming resentment, which leads to planning revenge and, ultimately, to a relapse.

I have days when I've written nothing, especially when working on my step four. 'Things' (healing or finding a job, for example) don't just happen. It takes patience, which is something a lot of recovering addicts, myself included, lack. An example of my impatience is when I decided to use my retractable washing line. The cord was all knotted. I tried for a short time with a screwdriver to get the knots out but had no success. Rather than persevering, I cut the end off and bought a new washing line that hooks onto three different places in the garden. I like the saying, 'It is what it is.' That's what I thought after I'd cut the old washing line.

I haven't experienced a feeling of success since I completed the drug and alcohol course while sober. Neither is experiencing feelings such as excitement, calm, contentment, happiness, hopefulness, and so on. I can honestly say that today I feel calm but tired, hopeful about the future, excited that this book might actually be a success, and happy about the healing that has begun with certain family members. Why would I want to lose these feelings? I don't, but I know they are only possible if I remain clean and sober, continue moving forward with gratitude, and thank God every day for bringing me to where I am today.

One of the things I *love* most about being sober is that I'm present for my kids and can answer the phone any time they call. I no longer have to lie with short texts listing reasons I can't speak to them. And more importantly, I don't need to drink over their problems. In the past, I would have made it all about me—poor me, how awful—and then drink. My kids are perfectly capable of managing their lives without me. I've had to realise that and stopped being a 'helicopter mum'. Yes, they need me and always will, in the same way I need and love my Mum, but they are just happy that I'm doing OK and making a life for myself.

My minister preached in church recently about the dangers of building our lives on sand. The scripture talks about how a wise man builds his house on solid ground and the unwise man builds his on sand. I relate this to my recovery. Steps one, two, and three are the firm foundation of a successful recovery, as is a belief in a higher power. I heard it said many times in Sydney AA meetings— 'One, two, three, *bust.*' What this means is that, if you don't persevere onto step four, you are on shaky ground. I knew that I was putting off all my step fours so much due to fear and shame; these emotions were preventing me from seeing the truth about myself.

I also heard a story years ago in the Baptist church I attended in Sydney. There was a raging flood. A man climbed to the roof of his house as the water rose and prayed he would be saved. A life raft came past. He refused to get in, as he trusted God would keep him safe. When a second raft came along, he again refused to get in. The water was up to his knees when he saw a rescue helicopter arrive. Again he refused to get in and asked God, 'Why aren't you saving me?' God replied, 'I sent those life rafts and helicopter.' I think, very often, we forget to realise how powerful God is and can ignore signals or messages from him. I have many times.

I believe I'm exactly where God wants me to be at this moment in time. He knew I was 'done', finished, beaten, on my last admission to rehab, and it is by his love and grace that I am alive and 'relatively' sane. I still have moments of madness, but they are getting fewer.

I have learnt a great deal about myself, and I think it's time to stop digging. Quite honestly, I've turned myself inside out, shined a torch on everything and everybody in my life. There is a time to stop digging, cease the moment, experiment with new things, dare to dream, and keep moving ahead, using all the tools you need for your recovery. I had been in early recovery several times, but this felt different. I've said this a few times, but it bears repeating: *I've stopped running.* It's true. When I look back over my life, I was always frantically trying to be the perfect daughter, sister, wife, mum, or friend. And in all of that self-inflicted chaos, I lost myself.

There is no excuse for my drinking. Nobody forced alcohol down my throat. But living with such high expectations of myself and others caused me to find solace in the bottle—well, many bottles, as my disease progressed. I knew this time had to be different. I'd dodged too many bullets and knew, if I relapsed again, I would be dead within weeks or maybe months—that, whatever the time period, I wouldn't make it back again.

In my first sobriety, I was always amazed as I watched people in restaurants sip wine, leave glasses half-full, and, worst of all, not take what was left in the bottle home! Good for them. They are not alcoholics. I would never have behaved like that, and as my drinking progressed, there were no more meals out. All my drinking was done behind locked and closed doors, blinds shut, phone on silent. And the only person who saw me take a drink in seven years was my daughter, when she caught me in the bathroom.

I went to stay with one of my best friends and my god-daughter for a week recently. It felt wonderful to be a part of her life just for a week. My friend was honest about the fear she had lived through, thinking she would find out I'd died. It was only a short conversation, and she in no way wanted me to feel guilty. She loves me unconditionally, as do I her. I was always up first and loved seeing her when she got up. We had a pretty lazy time. We watched films, chatted, and went grocery shopping. And I just loved being with both my friend and her daughter.

She came to an AA meeting with me. I filled her in about the format, as she'd never been to one before. The meeting was packed. We sat in the front row, and the meeting began with welcoming any newcomers, people who hadn't been to that meeting before, and anyone returning from a relapse. I said my name and explained I was from Wales. My friend said her name, that she was here to support me, and that she was concerned about her drinking, which was a slight white lie, as she barely drinks at all. I heard some powerful shares and halfway through the meeting felt pissed off that the meetings in my area were nothing like this. I missed the meetings in Sydney. At home, I barely saw any middle-aged mums like me in the meetings. And on the whole, NA and CA are where the young people are. So where are all the fifty-something alcoholic women? It's not for me to say, but I'm pretty sure they are drinking behind closed doors, life and themselves looking 'perfect'!

The rehab I'd been in has an after-care programme, every Wednesday evening between six thirty and eight o'clock. I was finally able to go. The lovely gay man who introduced me to smoking with a peg picked me up from my friend's and drove us to Worthing. It was lovely seeing him look so well. We chatted the entire time, had an early dinner, and arrived early at 6 p.m. We rang the doorbell. It took a while, but I heard the lovely older therapist who runs the group say, 'I bet that's S – – – –' (referring to me). It felt incredible to walk through the front door, the same one I had stumbled through drunk, desperate, and beaten eighty-nine days earlier. It was lovely seeing two of the caseworkers who knew me and six clients I had been in with on previous admissions. I gave the staff some chocolates and a packet of pegs—just a bit of fun, as I'd only used about three while in there. They laughed, and we all hugged.

While staying with my friend I finished reading the book Mum had given me a month previously, *Total Forgiveness: Achieving God's Greatest Challenge*, written by R. T. Kendall. It talked about what total forgiveness is and what it is not. The words 'God's Greatest Challenge' were not wrong. I was extremely challenged by this book and realised an essential part of my recovery was to forgive not only others but also myself. It is a well-known fact that 'resentments' are a number-one offender when it comes to relapsing. For me this is true, along with indescribable shame resulting from my words and actions. I can't even hazard a guess at the amount of hours resentments have festered and grown in my mind. Another gem I heard many times in AA with regard to hanging onto resentments was 'It's like drinking the poison and expecting the other person to die.' Spot on. While tormenting myself, plotting revenge, and wanting that person to suffer for what they did, they were probably carrying on with their own lives with no thought of the impact of their words or actions. I, on the other hand, would be all consumed, resulting in drinking the 'poison' and back to the hell of active addiction.

Baring in mind the previous paragraph, the following quotes at the beginning of *Total Forgiveness* made perfect sense. First, Nelson Mandela was asked many times how he emerged from all those years in prison without being bitter. His reply was simple: 'Bitterness only hurts yourself.' US President Bill Clinton once said, 'If you hate, you will give them your heart and mind. Don't give these two things away.' I discussed the book with my friend, and I loved her words of wisdom. 'Stop looking behind you,' she told me. 'You're not going that way.' Her advice was simple but very true.

I've also practised not being and doing things perfectly. An example, which is rather shallow but true, is when I painted my fingernails a few weeks ago. I smudged one on the kitchen bench. The old me would have redone it, but I decided to leave it. I can also leave the toilet roll holder empty and not have it always with three rolls on it. I don't over-order groceries, cleaning products, soft drinks, and so on online. I do one order a month for heavy goods and shop locally for fish, fruit, and veggies. These may sound like small things, but they were all part of needing to be in control and 'perfect'. I have a wicker basket in my bedroom with spare toiletries. When I opened it when I got home this time, I found eight tubes of toothpaste, six deodorants, five toothbrushes, three packets of facial wipes, two large boxes of cotton buds, and three pairs of exfoliating mittens. That should last me a while!

I flew to Edinburgh to have a long weekend with my kids. We had a wonderful time—going on sightseeing buses, visiting the castle, and walking for miles exploring this beautiful city. We had so much fun, but for me, the most precious thing was that my daughter didn't feel she had to stay with me in the hotel I was in. She trusted me, which was priceless. I had arrived drunk on my previous visit, convinced they wouldn't notice, which of course they did. It still amazes me how deluded I've been so many times, believing loved ones didn't know I was drinking. My daughter had stayed with me in the hotel, and out of desperation and my extreme love for them, I took large amounts of codeine in order to remain sober during my three days with them.

God has opened so many doors for me and put people in my path. Writing *Dying for a Drink* in such early recovery is a miracle. I believe God has guided me and protected my mind. He has helped me know when to stop typing when doing so became too painful.

We are all one drink or drug away from where we left off—from the last drink or the last time we used. I don't take things for granted. Each day is a blessing, and I thank God I am where I am. One of the biggest things I've done this time is reach out. I phone friends when I'm struggling. I keep in contact with six people I was in rehab programmes with, all of whom are still clean and sober. We text and chat. It's always lovely to hear how they are doing, and it encourages us all to keep on doing what we're doing to maintain our sobriety. I touched on the importance of staying safe earlier, and would like to add, I've had to cease contact with many people I've spent time within rehab or the drug and alcohol centre. Once I see (or suspect) they are drinking or using again, I can't allow myself to become involved in their chaos. Like many things, I've had to learn the hard way—this is no exception—but it is a vital way of protecting my sobriety and sanity.

My son recently spent a week in Spain on a field trip. He emailed me some of his pictures of fossils and rock formations. I am so thrilled he is finally studying something he is passionate about. I've said it before, but I'll say it again. The fact I am present for my kids—that I can answer the phone when they ring, be interested in their lives, and be there if they need me—is *priceless*.

I had a really bad throat infection recently. The first antibiotics didn't work, so I went and got a different type, which did work. The following Wednesday, my Mum popped into the charity shop and was told I was sick. There was a knock on the door at 10.30 a.m. It was Mum. She looked relieved to see me; I think, deep down, she may have worried I'd relapsed. This would be totally understandable. *Trust* is a massive topic; there are no set guidelines on when loved ones will trust us again. It may take months, years, or even forever.

I have cut down on my meetings now that I'm over four months clean and sober. I still go to three or four a week but do have a life outside AA. I know a lot of people make AA their lives, often going out for coffee and meals before or after meetings, which is fine, but it's not for me. I want to have a healthy balance in my life, and I do at the moment. I go into town four days a week for meetings and activities at the drug and alcohol centre, go to church on Sundays, and give myself permission to do nothing on Saturdays. Rest and taking time out for myself is a vital part of my recovery—it's part of self-care, which I lacked totally while drinking. For me, I include as part of my self-care the things I 'feed' my mind. I don't watch much TV, as I've been somewhat appalled by what's on since moving back. Reality shows that shame, ridicule, and disappoint people, making them feel totally inadequate, seem cruel and unnecessary. I choose to watch shows that leave me feeling good, for example, *Call the Midwife*. I haven't read a trashy magazine in years and am careful when it comes to listening to music. I used to torture myself with old 'soppy' playlists, longing to be back with my first husband—now that's pretty tragic! I don't want my life to be just about meetings, working the steps, and ringing other addicts. I want to start living, have some fun, and dream of my life to come. This is a far cry from how I was a year ago. I used to say my life was like *Groundhog Day* and that I was barely existing. But as my drinking progressed, it was far worse, and I felt *nothing*. When I did come to after a blackout, I would simply drink myself into another blackout.

I believe this is an action (not a reaction) programme. It's so easy to have a knee-jerk reaction to people or situations. But I'm learning to pause and think what my reaction, if any, should be. By action, I mean *action*. I cannot stand still in my recovery. That could be dangerous. Not being able to drive this winter has been a struggle. But I accept that and have, at times, had to force myself out of the door with numerous layers of clothing, a bobble hat, and gloves. It's been worth it. I've said before isolation and boredom are major blocks to recovery. I've made sure I've left the house every day and phoned people when I've been struggling.

AA, NA, CA, all the fellowships are spiritual programmes. For me, spirituality means continued connection with God and devotion to spiritual needs instead of worldly things. Spiritual things include unconditional loving, joy, patience, kindness, goodness, faithfulness, self-control, and humility. If I allow selfishness, resentment, dishonesty, and fear to be part of me, I block out spiritual things. I must be willing to peel away the layers of pain to expose the core. The seedlings of joy will sprout, and I will be able to feel joy, happiness, and hope again. Maintaining healthy boundaries is essential. I need to keep myself safe, protect my mind, and not allow people, places, and things to annoy me. Of course they will at times, but it's what I choose to do with those thoughts and feelings that counts.

I often look at customers in the charity shop and wonder what's going on in their lives. Are they sad? Lonely? We are all too often judged on the way we look and the jobs we do. For years, I was known as 'the wife' of my first husband. We would go to work functions, and I very rarely got asked anything about myself. The conversations were always work related.

I believe I lost my sense of identity a long time ago. It's only now that I'm starting to discover who I am and what I like doing.

One of my favourite hymns is 'Amazing Grace'. I am including here Chris Tomlin's lyrics (italics mine):

> Amazing grace
> How sweet the sound
> That saved a wretch like me
> I once was lost, but now I'm found
> Was blind, but now I see
> 'Twas grace that taught my heart to fear
> And grace my fears relieved
> How precious did that grace appear
> The hour I first believed
> *My chains are gone*
> *I've been set free*
> My God, my Saviour has ransomed me
> And like a flood His mercy rains
> Unending love, Amazing grace
> The Lord has promised good to me
> His word my hope secures
> He will my shield and portion be
> As long as life endures
> The earth shall soon dissolve like snow
> The sun forbear to shine
> But God, Who called me here below
> Will be forever mine
> Will be forever mine
> You are forever mine

I love the words in this hymn. 'Saved a wretch like me'—how wonderful. And if Jesus was walking on this earth today, he would bother with people like us. 'My chains are gone/I've been set free'. This is how I felt that day on the beach—that I had been set free form the bondage of alcohol and drugs and my unhealthy thoughts, feelings, and behaviours.

Our possibilities are only limited by what we can dream. Our daily routine can seem boring. Mine certainly has in the past. But think about how active addiction was—a life of misery, fear, resentments, anger, and self-hatred. The list goes on. I know that, for me, if I find myself in a pickle at some point in the day, I need to press the pause button, turn my will over to God, and start the day again.

A girlfriend rang me one day to see how I was, and I replied, 'OK.' That was the best I could do. In fact, I was more than OK. I was clean, sober, and not causing any more chaos or hurting my loved ones. So really, my response could have been, 'Bloody great.'

I was sick for a long time so cannot expect to be well in such a short time. My friend suggested I pat myself on the back for where I was now. I did, reluctantly. Hopefully, as I continue gaining strength, I shall be able (hand on heart be able) to say, 'Good on you' to myself and to realise my life is so precious—every waking moment of it. Yes, I've had and will have days when I feel tired, frustrated, and tempted to isolate. Those days, I surrender, accept I'm feeling 'off', and do something nice for myself, like cook my favourite meal or have a bubble bath. Then I bid that day farewell as 'not the best'.

One of my many favourite pieces of scripture is Jeremiah 29:11, which reads, '"For I know the plans I have for you," declares the Lord, "plans to prosper you and not harm you, plans to give you hope and a future."' My Mum often says her life is a journey with Jesus walking alongside her. I believe this has been and continues to be true for me. When I look back at all the near-death experiences I've escaped, I believe Jesus lay in that deep dark pit with me, cradled me, and gently lifted me up, held me tight, and gave me the courage to fight for my precious life. The two biggest miracles in my life are my son's recovery and the young man he is today and *me*, free from the obsession to drink or drug, and freedom from the bondage of self; by that, I mean 'It's not all about me.' It has been since my move back, and I'm not sure I'll ever fully comprehend the extent of fear, anger, disappointment, and despair my loved ones have endured. I shall continue to pray that God will heal their 'broken' minds and hearts caused by my drinking and that in his time these relationships will heal and trust will be restored.

My recovery may sound a bit too good to be true, and trust me, I often think that myself. Writing *Dying for a Drink* started off with reading old journals and trying to make sense of how my life had gone so horribly wrong. It's been extremely cathartic, but has also given me far better insight into 'me' and provided closure in many areas of my life.

Being financially privileged has allowed me to get into private rehabs, with one day's notice. I was incapable of making the decision to go, and I believe the loving interventions of my three best friends and first husband saved my life, for which I'll be eternally grateful. My Mum has often said to me, 'God will use where you've been to help others.' If, by some miracle, this book becomes a bestseller, I will invest the money in a rehab facility. I will buy a large old house in Swansea and hopefully get NHS approval. What a wonderful dream to have, a non-fee-paying rehab, where lives will (literally) be saved, where people will be detoxed properly and are given a safe place to learn how to live without alcohol or drugs. So many hospital beds are taken up by alcohol- or drug-related issues. We need more NHS rehab facilities. For me, to be a part of putting one in place would be the ultimate way of giving back.

I hope you have been able to identify with the similarities rather than the differences in my story and your own and that you realise there is hope and a life free from alcohol and drugs. We don't need them! I pray that reading this has given you the courage to tackle your addiction.

Lightning Source UK Ltd.
Milton Keynes UK
UKHW01f0311060718
325272UK00013B/211/P